REBIRTH
INTO
PURE LAND

❈ ❈ ❈

A True Story of Birth,
Death, and Transformation &
How We Can Prepare for
The Most Amazing Journey of Our Lives

❈ ❈ ❈

ROBERT SACHS

ISBN: 1470118505

ISBN-13: 9781470118501

Other books by Robert Sachs:

Perfect Endings: A Conscious Approach to Dying and Death

*Becoming Buddha: Awakening the Wisdom
and Compassion to Change your World*

The Passionate Buddha: Wisdom on Intimacy and Enduring Love

Wisdom of the Buddhist Masters: Common and Uncommon Sense

*Nine Star Ki: Feng Shui Astrology for Deepening Self-Knowledge
and Enhancing Relationships, Health, and Prosperity*

Tibetan Ayurveda: Health Secrets from The Roof of The World

Rebirth Into Pure Land

ROBERT SACHS

Dear Sharon,

The journey a opens
our heart...

In Spirit,
Robert Sachs
Apr. 2016

TABLE OF CONTENTS

FOREWORDS

"In the mystery of life and of death, there are more alternatives than imagination can conjure. This is the remarkable story of the grace that is our own great deathless nature and the grief, too, that even heaven cannot wholly eradicate.

This is a book of options, an honoring of the continuum that few have believed possible. It is a rare tale about the death of a child and the rebirth of the spirit in the hearts of all who were near - and the skillful passing into what is available to us all - our original nature."

Stephen Levine
Author of *Who Dies?*

"Robert Sachs accomplishes something unique with the personal narrative of this book. Through his attention to detail and a wide inclusion of birth and in circumstances at the time of death of his daughter Shamara and many others who he has sat with over the years, he catches and describes the often illogical but deeply human events at that critical time. Being compassionate, practical, and non-judgmental, what he describes dissolves many of the taboos about the recycling of our bodies. At the same time, from his experience of phowa, the Tibetan Buddhist practice of conscious dying, Robert adds the joyful underlying certainty that the richness of life will travel on as a stream of awareness and learn through our bodies and states of existence until it recognizes its timeless nature. *Rebirth Into Pure Land* is a very helpful book, bridging especially Judeo-Christian and Tibetan Buddhist practices. It is my wish that this work touches the life of many."

Lama Ole Nydahl

Author of *The Way Things Are*

INTRODUCTION

When our daughter, Shamara Phillipa, died on January 17th, 1984 at 48-days of age of Sudden Infant Death Syndrome (SIDS), my world changed. Assumptions of what it meant to be a father, a husband, and health care provider, as well as my view of what life was about and might have in store for me came crashing down. In their place emerged an unexpected direction. An expression of that change of heart and direction came in my desire to share the remarkable events that – upon hindsight – led up to, occurred during, and have continued to unfold since her passing. Over the years, I have come to see that the passing of people in our lives has this impact on us all, one way or the other, sometimes in small ways, other times profound. Of all of life's events, death is the most humbling and seems to be one of our best teachers on how to live and love more fully.

Shamara's death of SIDS did not happen in what some might call ordinary circumstances. She died while a Buddhist meditation teacher was visiting us. And, as a master and teacher of the conscious dying practices of Tibet, known as *phowa* (pronounced poh-wha), this teacher, Lama Ole Nydahl, used this extraordinary spiritual practice to effect what in medical terms can only be described as miracles. It was then that I learned that it is possible to help in and even transform the dying process. In what most of us in the West would define as being a time of utter hopelessness, something can be done. And having witnessed this to be true, I have devoted myself to learning more and sharing with others what they can do to prepare for and consciously work with their own dying and that of their loved ones.

In its first edition, *Rebirth Into Pure Land* inspired many friends and strangers. I am always a bit dubious when someone says, "This book will change your life." But in the case of telling Shamara's story, after watching, listening to, and receiving letters from countless people over the last fifteen years since the story was first released, I must honestly say that, yes, hearing Shamara's story will change your life. It will change how you see life and, more than likely, how you live your life.

Rebirth was initially written more as a memoir and how my family's practice of Buddhist meditation and philosophy impacted our view and state of mind in Shamara's passing. Although I was happy to see it published, I was still a religious neophyte and did not see or make any attempts to really venture beyond the enclaves of my own spiritual community. But, 27 years later, having seen how her story has touched people from all faiths and walks of life, and my subsequent years of study, training, and practice in methods of conscious dying as part of my own personal development along with my profession as a hospice social worker and bereavement counselor, I felt it was time to, once again, share Shamara's story. And, I wanted to offer the techniques and perspectives I have seen that make it possible for each and every one of us to traverse this inevitable time in a manner that prepares us ahead of time, serves us during our passing, and helps even those we leave behind. My goal is to inspire all who read this new edition of *Rebirth into Pure Land* to embrace death and learn that it is actually possible to work with the dying process, even death itself, as a natural part of our living.

Of course, the death of a baby is always sad. But in this new version, *Rebirth Into Pure Land* invites you to step back from this human tragedy, see the power, mystery, joy and miraculous possibilities in the sacred and remarkable world of which we all are a part, and even be an active participant until our final moments. As Stephen Levine says in the Foreword, *Rebirth Into Pure Land,* offers each of us options. When we become conscious of and engage our intentions on any process that we are going through, many possibilities can spontaneously arise in how to best address the moment. As such, *Rebirth Into Pure Land* points us towards every moment of our living.

Inevitably, no matter what road we take, in the impermanence of it all, we shall all arrive at the same final destination. Other than the numerous miracles that we witnessed in Shamara's death and transformation and the many feelings of presence my wife and I are sometimes in touch with and other times not, her legacy and my intention for writing is to provide inspiration and tools to make it possible for each and every one of us to take the same amazing journey that Shamara, herself, took.

Considering that each one of us dies, as a culture, we don't handle dying or death very well. It is almost as if we are afraid that if we talk about it, we are beckoning it towards us. We try to hide it from our children and our youth learn about it from the street or media in real or Hollywood versions more often than having serious, honest discussion at home. Even though all of us know in some place in our minds as we get older that death is a truth that we cannot escape, we tend to turn the dying and death processes over to medical experts, who seem to be infected with an ethos that makes death the enemy; something to deny, fight, and only acquiesce to. And, once our medicines and heroic methods "fail," only then do our religious traditions come in, maybe offer a sacrament or final blessing, but spend most efforts on comforting the bereaved. There is little in our traditions that understands or tries to work with the dying process itself other than in a pastoral way.

Death happens at any age. It happens quickly for some, slowly for others and the process can come painlessly in the night or rage at us in searing agony day after day. In my book, Perfect Endings, I contend that dying and death come to us in accordance with how we have lived. Being a hospice social worker, bereavement counselor, volunteer, I have observed that the degree to which we do not embrace dying as a part of life is the degree to which our working with the dying and bereaved falls woefully short of creating healthy spiritual growth and psychological and philosophical integration of the death and legacy of our love ones into our lives. That is why it does not comes as a surprise that whereas Medicare provides for a six-month hospice benefit for those diagnosed with a terminal illness, because both doctors and families struggle with and are in denial of the dying they are witnessing before them, the norm is for people to use six weeks or less of that benefit. In the same way our culture does not teach or encourage us much in the way of self-reflection in our own lives and experiences, save for the conscience our faiths encourage us to have, when it comes to our own dying, we wait too long and the result is a panic that blurs our abilities to make clear decisions on any number of end-of-life issues, especially the most important one; creating a sane and supportive environment in which we can die in a peaceful and conscious manner.

But, this brings us to another issue within our culture. Dying well: Does it really matter?

On this, our religious traditions are divided. All will agree that it is much better to be at peace and out of pain as we die. This is a testament to our natural compassion. But, regardless of whether this is a reality or not, our perspectives on what happens next seem not to be connected to nor are somehow shaped by the attitudes and intentions we put into dying itself. It remains a hopeless condition which we hope will go well, but then whether it does or not, there is whatever happens next. And on this point, our various faiths take a wide range of positions. Some teach that when we die, there is nothing or that we just become dust; end of story. Others say that our final destination is a heaven or hell, depending on what we have done, whether we believe, how strongly we believe, or have been born again ensuring our safe passage to the destination of our choosing. In keeping with this perspective, there are some new agers who say that this life is their last; that they are never coming back. Although popular polling would indicate that a good number of people have a private belief in reincarnation, no modern western faith embraces this as a possibility, let alone reality. Sure, there are people who have had near death experiences who describe what they have seen "on the other side." There may be stories of children recalling previous lives and demonstrating their knowledge of such. Most convincing of all in such stories is embodied by His Holiness the Fourteenth Dalai Lama; one of the many lamas of Tibet who recall their previous lives and demonstrate a remarkable ability to not only remember incidents, but also carry on teachings they have learned in previous lives into their current one. It may be easy to dismiss the "other side" crowd and children as just having flights of fantasy and that the information they present as mere coincidental. It is harder to apply this attitude to one of the most revered spiritual leaders of our time.

But, the tradition that the Dalai Lama practices and teaches, the Tantric Buddhism of Tibet, looks at reincarnation as a rather cosmic recycling program. Born with the potential to be as a Buddha from the very start, our original condition is that of being basically good. We have all we will ever need to reach our true potential as a being of light; i.e. enlightened, if we learn and practice methods to accomplish this. And, we have a relentless urge towards light that continues through to its full realization from one lifetime to the next. This process is not an inevitable linear trajectory. We learn as we go and sometimes we falter in various ways. We will end up in happy and painful lives and realms of existence. We may even go in and out of various heavens and hells as we progress. But, in the end, if we see ourselves as spiritual beings having a human experience, if we try to become and remain as conscious as we possibly can in each and every experience and milestone in our lives, then we all will eventually arrive at the most lasting of destinations; in a state of awakeness, of total oneness in the full awareness of our inter-connectedness. In short, we all become Buddhas.

But, of course, that is what I believe. And that said, does learning methods to prepare oneself to die and understanding and supporting the mental and physical states of the dying process matter if you don't believe in reincarnation?

To this I say, YES, it does matter. It matters because in our lives, we are taught that information is power. We are taught that if we practice anything consistently, that when we are no longer practicing but are in the process of doing, we will do that much better. We shall make instinctual or habitual that which we have trained ourselves to do over and over. Thus, in times that are stressful, even dire, there is a greater probability that these instincts will kick in and support us. Applying this to dying and death, if in what most of us would agree is the most dire moment in our lives we knew that we could focus our minds and prepare our bodies for us to die with less pain and in greater peace, regardless of whether you believe in an afterlife or not, wouldn't anyone want to do what it takes?

That is the point of each of the methods and techniques I shall share in this book. And, this is the deeper message underlying the story you are about to read about our daughter, Shamara Phillipa, and her passing into a Pure Land, the concept of which you will come to understand in the story's telling..

Rebirth Into Pure Land has three distinct parts. In Part One, I offer you the story of Shamara in the language and energy I wrote it originally. As mentioned earlier, it takes place within the context of Buddhist spiritual practice and in the lives of myself and my beloved wife, Melanie.   Whilst we have always strived to integrate the Buddhist way of living and being in the world into our contemporary Western lives, because the events occurred within the context of such practice and philosophy, it has been unavoidable, and at the same time, seems important to include some of the Sanskrit and Tibetan words associated with the practice. I feel that the story itself is so powerful that the use of such terminology will not weaken its impact. And, for the curious, I have created a glossary. Anyone who wants to learn more about the words - how they are pronounced and what they mean - can do so.

By the same token, the method that was used in Shamara's death, process known as the yoga of *phowa*, translated from the Tibetan as translated as the transference of consciousness at the moment of death is recounted in the context of our Buddhist world view.   But, it can be used by anyone of any faith who wants to more consciously liberate themselves or be liberated into a more positive state or place beyond this world. In time, it is my belief that neuroscience and our understanding of the subtle aspects of the dying process and what happens with consciousness after it leaves the body and migrates to its next destination will be proven out in advances in medical and scientific methodologies and eventually have a language of its own distinct from the current Buddhist explanations I present here.

I have also written this account as an acknowledgement of the remarkable people who played a part in these events; friends, teachers, even strangers, who stepped forward without hesitation to help, support and play their part in the events and miracles of those times. Many of them remain close and dear to us. Others have moved on in their lives as we have moved on in ours. Even so, I wish to re-kindle my honoring of such friends and acquaintances.

In Part Two, I shall outline the dying and death process as explained in the tradition of Ayurvedic and Chinese medicine as well as the Buddhist understanding of each of the stages we go through in that process. For the most part, we are not use to thinking of health or any our life events within the context of systems, thus any system offered would seem foreign to us. Thus, I have tried to present in simple and straight forward terms the systems of health care and mind training that have been best codified, outlined, and preserved over the centuries. The goal is to provide you with invaluable information to help you become more through the dying process. Knowledge IS power and knowing this information will empower you to more effectively manage your own death as well as the death of others you encounter over the course of your remaining life.

The second chapter of Part Two will supplement this information with an actual exercise that you can practice in preparation for that time. It also provides you with a psycho-spiritual process to help you awaken to various dimensions of your physical and emotional experience here and now. Anyone practicing or wishing to embark upon a contemplative and meditative path or practice will find comfort, insight, and benefit from this exercise.

Part Three is devoted to more practical matters in the dying process; coping with pain, changes in consciousness, working with diet and massage, and ways of enhancing and safeguarding the moments during vulnerable moments in the dying process and when the outer pulse may have ceased, but still so much is happening internally with our body and mind, especially at a spiritual level. These recommendations come from a number of traditions as well as my own observations and experiences being with the dying.

What will be the end result of you reading and practicing what *Rebirth Into Pure Land* offers?

Because each and every one of us dies, the stories and methods shared here are for everybody. At the same time, most of us would prefer not to die alone. We would like friends and loved ones to be with us, for comfort and support. In a time when most of us feel powerless to do anything of value to help our dying friend or loved one, the exercises and methods taught here will help you to act as spiritual midwife through the final transformation we go through in this current

INTRODUCTION

When our daughter, Shamara Phillipa, died on January 17th, 1984 at 48-days of age of Sudden Infant Death Syndrome (SIDS), my world changed. Assumptions of what it meant to be a father, a husband, and health care provider, as well as my view of what life was about and might have in store for me came crashing down. In their place emerged an unexpected direction. An expression of that change of heart and direction came in my desire to share the remarkable events that – upon hindsight – led up to, occurred during, and have continued to unfold since her passing. Over the years, I have come to see that the passing of people in our lives has this impact on us all, one way or the other, sometimes in small ways, other times profound. Of all of life's events, death is the most humbling and seems to be one of our best teachers on how to live and love more fully.

Shamara's death of SIDS did not happen in what some might call ordinary circumstances. She died while a Buddhist meditation teacher was visiting us. And, as a master and teacher of the conscious dying practices of Tibet, known as *phowa* (pronounced poh-wha), this teacher, Lama Ole Nydahl, used this extraordinary spiritual practice to effect what in medical terms can only be described as miracles. It was then that I learned that it <u>is</u> possible to help in and even transform the dying process. In what most of us in the West would define as being a time of utter hopelessness, something can be done. And having witnessed this to be true, I have devoted myself to learning more and sharing with others what they can do to prepare for and consciously work with their own dying and that of their loved ones.

In its first edition, *Rebirth Into Pure Land* inspired many friends and strangers. I am always a bit dubious when someone says, "This book will change your life." But in the case of telling Shamara's story, after watching, listening to, and receiving letters from countless people over the last fifteen years since the story was first released, I must honestly say that, yes, hearing Shamara's story will change your life. It will change how you see life and, more than likely, how you live your life.

Rebirth was initially written more as a memoir and how my family's practice of Buddhist meditation and philosophy impacted our view and state of mind in Shamara's passing. Although I was happy to see it published, I was still a religious neophyte and did not see or make any attempts to really venture beyond the enclaves of my own spiritual community. But, 27 years later, having seen how her story has touched people from all faiths and walks of life, and my subsequent years of study, training, and practice in methods of conscious dying as part of my own personal development along with my profession as a hospice social worker and bereavement counselor, I felt it was time to, once again, share Shamara's story. And, I wanted to offer the techniques and perspectives I have seen that make it possible for each and every one of us to traverse this inevitable time in a manner that prepares us ahead of time, serves us during our passing, and helps even those we leave behind. My body that we occupy. Other than the amazing changes that can be effected for the dying, just offering such a service to the dying can be, in itself, amazing.

Several people helped to technically bring the first edition of this book together. Thanks go to Nancy Reinstein for typing, Susan Biggs for editorial comments, Lisa Graff for her cover design and Margaret Thompson, the editor and owner of Zivah Publishers who first brought this book out. Thanks also go to Lisa Hanaway and to Sidney Piburn of Snow Lion Publications for their encouragement, and of course, my wife and partner, Melanie who has been there throughout, helped in every aspect and lovingly reminded me when memory failed.

The title of this book, *Rebirth Into Pure Land*, has two meanings.

In literal Buddhist terms, it has to do with the death of our daughter, Shamara, and her subsequent rebirth into the Western Pure Land of the Amitabha Buddha - as confirmed by Phowa master, Lama Ole Nydahl and my beloved teacher, the Venerable Khenpo Karthar Rinpoche.

It is also about how these events revealed to us a sacred vision of reality. This vision has become the wellspring from which Melanie and I have continued to practice and commit ourselves to the teachings of the Buddha and have striven to integrate these teachings into every aspect of our being through our thoughts, words, actions and accomplishments. Our purpose and joy in life is to support others in deepening their own spiritual lives in any way we can to see this vision as well.

PART ONE:

REBIRTH INTO PURE LAND

CHAPTER ONE

PREPARATION

As human beings, we have never lost our awe for the sacredness of the two most pivotal milestones of our life; the coming and passing away of life. Viewed as isolated moments, one might easily just note them as biological events. But, each seems carried on a stream; a stream that courses through the other, lesser comings and goings that we spend most of our time focused on. If we were able to stand on the banks of the stream rather than contend with the currents while we are in their midst, it might just be possible for us to see that the coming and going of life always lets us know of their arrival much sooner than we have previously imagined. And, I would venture to say that because this is so, when the perfection of birth and death arrive, the vague understanding of this as true that we may only intuit in the back of our minds gives us cause to reflect. The awe of the moment pushes back the boundaries of time and space as we stand witness to the magnificence of it all.

In the case of the birth of our daughter, Shamara, it took me eight years of standing on the banks to begin to understand what her coming to and passing from us meant in the moment and how it would shape our lives to this day. It took me eight years to write what you are about to read.

In mid-August of 1983 I returned home to Lexington, Kentucky after spending some precious time with my spiritual teacher, the Venerable Khenpo Karthar Rinpoche, in Woodstock, New York and in Boston with the Michio Kushi, the main teacher of the Macrobiotic diet and lifestyle movement in the West. From Michio I was able to bring back a great deal of useful information for the physician whose holistic health clinic I worked in. From Khenpo Rinpoche, I returned with practical ways to dissolve illusion as well as a promise from him to come to teach in Lexington in the late fall.

I had driven the 17 hours straight from upstate New York to be with Melanie, the inspiration in my life, and our two daughters, Kai and Tina. I was both exhausted and elated. In the days that followed, Melanie and I would sort out all the pieces of the trip. With the news that Khenpo Rinpoche wanted to visit Lexington there was suddenly a lot more to do.

In fact, there was a lot to do anyway. There was getting back to work and being on a schedule. There was the daily running of the house, the garden and two very busy little girls. Kai was about to enter kindergarten and Tina, a Montessori pre-school. And Melanie was 5 months pregnant.

We normally found ourselves busy, dealing with our immediate family and home life and a circle of friends with whom we connect wherever we live - people who want to share in the knowledge we have made a point of gathering for the sole purpose of passing on to others. Inviting Khenpo Rinpoche to Lexington – to a city and group of people who had never before seen a Tibetan high lama - only intensified what we were doing. There was a deeper feeling of responsibility, as well as a keen awareness that with his visit, we ourselves would also be more in the public eye.

And then there was Melanie's pregnancy, ongoing and ever changing in the midst of all these daily and special events. The pregnancy of this, our third child together, made us quite introspective. Perhaps our state of introspectionwas because the conception of the child had come about as a part of a process of healing some old wounds which had kept Melanie and I estranged for a time. But there seemed to be more to it. The constant motion of our lives and demands on our time made it difficult to pinpoint exactly what it was we were feeling. We felt like we were moving through something together. On the one hand, feeling together in this way was reassuring. On the other, each day presented us with an uncertainty that we had not experienced before.

During the week, I was at work with my friends at the Holistic Medical Center. I was writing out the material from my Boston visit with Michio Kushi and seeing clients one after another. I spent my evenings and weekends building a meditation and shrine room in the attic space of our house in preparation for Khenpo Rinpoche's visit. Melanie, meanwhile, was busy getting our daughters off to school, tending the garden and preparing the house for Rinpoche's visit and the expected early winter arrival of our newest family member. In her "spare" time she was teaching cooking classes and organizing publicity schedules of volunteers for Khenpo Rinpoche's visit. In these months, we spoke at meals, talked over details on the phone and saw each other only briefly before exhaustion overcame us at night. Not much time to reflect - just do.

Doing what we do, being how we are, we certainly had the community buzzing! We have always enjoyed creating meaningful events for friends wherever we live. And in Lexington, we were involved in the growing Tibetan Buddhist community. We brought large groups of friends and fellow Buddhist practitioners to celebrate Tibetan New Year and other special sacred holidays. And, whenever we could we hosted our dear Buddhist teacher and brother, Ole Nydahl, and his wife, Hannah, in their whirlwind teaching circuits across America.

Ole had come to visit us every year since our time together in Woodstock, New York during the visit of the highest of all the living Tibetan lamas, His Holiness The Sixteenth Gyalwa Karmapa's (the longest line of reincarnate Tibetan masters, in his sixteenth incarnation) to America in 1980. Ole has an almost contagious energy which inspires enthusiasm for healthy spiritual practice. He has often been the front runner and ground breaker for the great Tibetan teachers to come to new locations where welcoming and like-minded friends are eager to connect with their true nature.

And now, our own teacher, the spiritual grandfather of our children, was coming to Lexington. The community's sense of wonder, appreciation and desire to be part of this local, historic event was both touching and inspiring.

4

Peter Blunt prepared a wooden platform for a throne. Ed Baker came by to help tape the sheet rock in the shrine room. Dick Levine and Anne Frye arranged for him to teach at the University of Kentucky.

Other friends volunteered to work and clean during the visit; Laurel Thatcher, Mara Genthner, Adelle Prager, Mrs. Govinda Rajalu, to name a few. And then there were our "guardian angels," Geoff and Diana Bullington, who arranged for a public talk. Geoff and Di have always been in the background for us. They were the first couple I met when I was invited by physician and friend Walt Stoll, to come to the Holistic Medical Center in Lexington to teach foot reflexology. Geoff and Di used their truck to help us with the move to Lexington from Columbus. We lived with them while we looked around for a house in town. They became our daughters' honorary aunt and uncle. Geoff and Di remain in our hearts as practical guides in the ways of spirit beyond any dogmatic allegiance to this or that school or tradition. And the time of our preparing for Khenpo Rinpoche, the bond that Melanie and I have with Geoff and Di was to become most apparent in the months that followed.

And then there was the pregnancy. We had always done home births for our children and saw no reason to make an exception this time. We were fortunate in that one of the best midwives in the region, Noni Rhodes, lived one street over. Our daughter, Kai, and Noni's daughter, Kelly, were the closest of friends. Melanie already spent much of her mom-to-mom, friend-to-friend time with Noni. Now she met with Noni and her partner, Debbie Neal, on a regular schedule for prenatal check-ups. And by all reports, Melanie was in perfect condition for the baby and all indicators pointed to an equally healthy baby inside, waiting for its time to arrive.

Along with Noni and Debbie, there was the support of my friend and colleague, Walt Stoll, a remarkable physician who was a pioneer advocate of holistic and preventive health care in America. Walt was charismatic and sometimes a bit "overly direct" with clients, media or whomever he felt needed to hear what he had to say. His bluntness some-times daunted Melanie. But in us, Walt could see a couple committed to health standards and ways of living that he both admired and aspired to. He did routine checks on Melanie throughout the pregnancy and, as a colleague and friend, was both honored and excited to attend Melanie's delivery - and be emergency backup if needed.

In addition to the professional support we had for the impending birth, many friends came forward in various helpful ways. The energy that Melanie and I had been giving to the community was being returned in kind by friends who eagerly awaited the arrival of our newest family member.

We were feeling, at once, caught up in our respective whirlwinds of activity and extremely blessed. The time was intense and action packed. There was a sense of joy and anticipation. And, there seemed an even greater force moving events along; something more powerful and extraordinary beyond our plans, moving us toward a time which had a deeper and as yet hidden message for us.

CHAPTER TWO

THE VISIT

One month almost to the day before Melanie's due date, Khenpo Rinpoche was on his way from Columbus, Ohio to Lexington.

Of course, the timing of preparation for his visit was down to the last minute. Final touches on the shrine room were done the night before. The gaps in the cooking, cleaning and interview schedules were filled in that day as well. With everything as organized as it can be before such a visit, there was the usual calm before the storm.

When a great spiritual master comes for a visit, there is a seemingly endless list of details which need attention. In the presence of greatness, especially those with great spiritual power and compassion, our experience has taught us that the left brain or organizational mind seems to go on vacation once they arrive. To avoid going crazy, we have learned to plan what we can with the full recognition that everything has its own timing and that such a teacher is more attuned to that clock than to the one on the wall. One learns to plan and then let go.

In those moments before Rinpoche's arrival, there was an extraordinary mixture of qualities: clarity, anxiety and fuzzy-headedness from all the late nights. And, for Melanie, there were Braxton Hicks contractions - a type of contraction that some women get during the latter stages of pregnancy. Their frequency and intensity appeared to be proportional to the degree she found herself overdoing in her preparations and tending to far too much.

In keeping with my own neurotic behavior, the thought of abandoning my incessant anticipatory pacing coincided with Rinpoche's arrival. And, in the first moments of seeing him, Melanie and I watched our attention to our daily lives give way to the single-minded purpose of serving him and all those who awaited his presence in our community.

Since it was the first time he had visited this particular house of ours, we took Rinpoche and his translator (and our good friend), Ngodrup Burkhar, up to our attic to see the shrine room. Freshly painted in sky blue, it was as if the whole room opened to the heavens. Rinpoche liked it, especially the sloping ceilings which met the walls at a height of three feet and six inches. Sitting around the edge of the room, one had to remind oneself not to get up too quickly, lest one bang one's head on the ceiling. Rinpoche said that this was good as it helped people to stay mindful.

Upon seeing the shrine and the throne, he must have quickly developed some plans. For as soon as he was settled into his living quarters, Ngodrup approached me with a shopping list. In no time, he and I were doing what is so customary to a lama or Rinpoche's visit - shopping.

First on the list was to get a large, ornate frame for a picture of His Holiness, the 16th Karmapa. Then we were off to a toy store to get gifts for our children and the children of friends who would visit. And we were also instructed to get some play dough. I did not know why play dough was such a priority but I soon learned of its great potential in Tibetan Buddhist ritual.

After Rinpoche settled in and the shopping was completed, the week passed in a magical way. Evening talks brought the interested and curious from around the state to Lexington. All of our friends from the local Dharmadhatu meditation center were there, as well as friends from the Zen and holistic health communities and others to whom we would grow closer over the remainder of our years in Lexington.

A weekend of meditation instruction and practice gave new students the opportunity to learn from a true master and old students the opportunity to experience deeper and richer dimensions to their practice and a greater appreciation for one of the four great traditions of Tibetan Buddhism; the Kagyu Lineage.

The movement in and through our house was continuous; friends were dropping off food, cleaning, having interviews with Rinpoche. It is in those times that one is functioning like the great saint, Chenrezig (or Loving Eyes), with 1,000 arms and several sets of eyes. Amidst it all I would watch Melanie, going through contractions, handling the crowds, growing more radiant each day in the field of Rinpoche's kindness and the natural, magical glow that a woman emanates as the day of birthing approaches.

Melanie had done a brilliant job of arranging the house to suit Rinpoche's needs and the continuous daily traffic of events. She had decided that the only place she could not straighten up was the basement.

And, in keeping with the way of such events, Khenpo Rinpoche spent much of his spare time in the basement cutting small pieces of wood for reasons that would gradually come to light.

Other precious moments between events and resting would find him in a rocking chair in his room with one or the other of our daughters on his lap while he fed them grapes, cookies and candies. The love and care he has shown them over the years has given the purest teaching on who the Buddha is and what the Dharma offers. Even in their rebellious teen years, our daughters have always gotten excited with the prospect of seeing him.

Rarely is there time to reflect with people on their interviews during the visit but a few friends had remarkable experiences that they wanted to share. Our friend and birthing doctor, Walt, who has great clarity in seeing auras and energy fields, reported to us that in coming to and leaving his interview, he could see large beams of light radiating from our attic shrine room where Rinpoche sat.

When one hosts a teacher, it is not uncommon to find that there is little private time with him to ask specific, personal questions. This indeed was the case in this visit. However, in hindsight, we realized that there was one aspect of our conversations with Rinpoche where there was a rather obvious omission. He never brought up Melanie's pregnancy and the impending birth. We later came to know that Tibetans are very family oriented. Births and children are celebrated. We have seen Rinpoche before and since that visit around expectant mothers. We have always observed his excitement and seen how he has given blessings to them for the birth. In the midst of his kindness and spiritual energy, this omission in our interactions and conversations with him was not noted by either Melanie or me.

But Rinpoche obviously knew more than he was prepared to say - at least to us. For, as we later learned, in his interview with our two "guardian angels" Geoff and Diana, Rinpoche made what seemed to them a rather odd but urgent request. He asked them to take care of us over the next few months. This was said in confidence and we only learned of these remarks when it became clear to Geoff and Di what Rinpoche had seen with his pure vision but would only allude to in their interview.

Rinpoche left a permanent mark in the hearts of our friends and on the soul of Lexington, Kentucky. A Karma Kagyu Dharma study group was established in our attic at that time. He had demonstrated to us through his direct kindness, teaching and simple, yet skillful means how our minds can transform even the most mundane feelings, perceptions and objects into sources of pure inspiration. He had shown us a spiritual realm worth taking refuge in. Even play dough and wooden sticks became transformed into shrine offerings worth venerating. Indeed, our entire neighborhood had been transformed into a Pure Land.

And perhaps it is in the radiance of this perception that all of what was to transpire in the months to come took place.

CHAPTER THREE

THE BIRTH

It takes about one week to catch up on sleep and reorient oneself to everyday affairs after such visits. At the same time, the intensity of Rinpoche's visit seemed to blend into our preparation for Melanie's birthing. People who had made themselves available to us and were experiencing the blessing of Khenpo Rinpoche were now available to help out with these preparations. And the momentum and excitement around this imminent event began to infect everyone around us.

Our friends gave Melanie an elaborate baby shower - the magnitude of which we had not experienced before the birth of either Kai or Tina. What was most striking to Melanie about this event was how profoundly generous, almost to the point of extravagance, people were with their gift offerings. At first we thought that perhaps our friends were simply expressing their appreciation to us for bringing Khenpo Rinpoche and his teachings to them. However, Melanie's sense was that it was as if they were preparing to honor someone very special who was getting ready to enter their lives.

Beyond this "regal" shower, the support group of professionals who were to assist us before, during and after Melanie's labor and delivery was pulling together in a very powerful, focused and somewhat surprising manner. A macrobiotic acquaintance I had made in Boston during my visit with Michio Kushi appeared and offered himself as cook to help Melanie during and after labor. David was wild, but as a macrobiotic cook focusing on strengthening and healing, he was a genius. Midwives Noni and Debbie and even our physician, Walt, were expressing their excitement. The fact that a physician and two midwives were all willing to attend the birth and work together was a bit unusual in itself.

And yet, in the midst of all this activity, Melanie and I felt quite sober. We had gone through births before and had felt the full range of emotions that such events evoke. However, this time was different. We did not know exactly why it was different, but every fiber of our being was telling us to be quiet, to be open and to listen.

On December 1, 1983, Melanie woke up, fed the children and walked Kai to school. As she was returning home she felt unusually quiet. She wasn't sure just what was going on. She decided to go over to Noni's for a cup of tea and while there called me. She just wanted to chat and then go on home. Upon hearing her voice, my intuition told me to tell her to get checked by Noni. In fact, at this point, she was already through most of the first stages of labor.

When I arrived home, Melanie was already there and home birth preparations were in full swing. While we have had midwives and physicians either present or to back us up, I have always been the primary birth attendant; being with Melanie through all the stages of labor, giving her massages, letting her vent herself through whatever labor has taken her into.

It is a sacred event where only truth resides and egos are not welcome.

What was so unusual about her labor this time was that Melanie was much quieter and much more focused than she had been in the past. If she was experiencing any discomfort at all, it seemed, from an observer's perspective, to be insignificant in light of whatever else she was going through internally as transition arrived.

By this time all the participants had arrived - except for one, of course. Walt was with us, along with Noni and Debbie. We had sent friends to retrieve Kai and Tina from school. And there was David, who prepared liquids and nourishment throughout.

Melanie's waters broke to low guttural sounds that she drew forth from deep within herself. She showed no signs of anguish, just an expression of deep concentration and the resolve to allow herself to be the portal through which our child would emerge to find a welcome home. It was not long from the time that Melanie entered transition that our daughter came silently into the world. And, as is customary for Melanie and me, the first sounds we spoke to her were the syllables of the mantra of Karmapa - KARMAPA CHENO.

Once the umbilical cord stopped pulsating, it was cut. Then the midwives bathed our daughter and lay her close to Melanie. Kai and Tina cuddled around their new sister. David stood by silently. Walt was moved to tears. Later he told us that in his 20 years experience as a physician he had never been to any birth like the one he had just witnessed. Melanie and I have always tried to make a sacred ritual of the births of our children. And this one was no exception. But beyond this, there was another quality present - something new, something serene - and perhaps that was what Walt was sensing.

Melanie and I never think of names for our children prior to their birth. It is our belief that, upon arrival, the child will let us know what it wishes to be called. It took about two hours for us to realize that our new daughter was to be called Shamara Phillipa Sachs.

Her middle name, Phillipa, was in memory of my favorite uncle who had recently passed away. Shamara was a derivation of the name of a high Tibetan teacher, Kunzig Shamar Rinpoche, with whom we had had the unique opportunity to spend time with when he first came to Columbus, Ohio.

Our first encounter with Shamar Rinpoche was unique in the sense that it was both informal and personal. He came to the meditation center in Columbus soon after His Holiness Karmapa had visited. No one had met him and no one really knew who he was. Because of this, people had not prepared for his arrival and they asked Melanie and me if we would be available to let him into the center and make him feel comfortable. Few of the high teachers speak good English. He was one who did and it was remarkable to have a complete afternoon serving him and being able to talk to him about practice, our experiences with His Holiness the Karmapa and whatever else came to mind. What was most striking to me in our conversations was the feeling that I was continuing prior conversations and receiving further clarification on questions I had discussed with His Holiness. It was as though it was the same mind in a different body. Shamar Rinpoche feels most like and reminds me of Karmapa and to this day he is my spiritual advisor .

In the days that followed, Shamar Rinpoche got to know our entire family. He commented on the unique qualities of our second daughter, Tina, and we told him that His Holiness had asked us to contact him in Sikkim upon her birth. He then sent her Dharma name to us through Ponlop Rinpoche. To this day she has a strong connection to the Dharma and a profound appreciation for practice.

As for my connection to Shamar Rinpoche, I had the unusual and auspicious opportunity to be given personal instruction on the nature of mind in the backyard of the center, alone with him. Such opportunities as this have always been rare and, with the increased demands upon and busier schedules of the Rinpoches and other lamas, are becoming even more so.

Perhaps that is why, two-and-one-half years later, without having seen or communicated with him through any conventional means, my mind turned to him as an inspiration when naming our daughter. In the hours that followed her birth, the significance of her name and the connection we had to Shamar Rinpoche became magically apparent.

Once Melanie had had a few hours in which to eat, get settled with Shamara and rest, we decided to call the main monastery of the Kagyu lineage in

America, Karma Triyana Dharmachakra (KTD) in Woodstock where Khenpo Karthar Rinpoche resided. We wanted to tell him of Shamara's birth and request a Dharma name for her. It was late afternoon, so I knew that the KTD office was closed. Still, I had the office manager, Pat Cliett's, home number.

When I got Pat on the phone, I told him about the birth and asked if he could request from Rinpoche a name for Shamara. Although I cannot recall verbatim what he said next, the message was clear. "Well," Pat replied, "I can get hold of Khenpo Rinpoche if you like. But Shamar Rinpoche has just unexpectedly arrived here. I could ask him."

It would have taken an act of extreme stupidity on my part to somehow not see such an obvious auspicious coincidence. Without hesitation, I asked Pat to please do this for us and Shamara. Roughly one week later, a special Dharma card arrived from Shamar Rinpoche with our daughter's name and his Dharma emblem. By then he had left Woodstock. However, I wanted to call Pat to thank him for his efforts on our behalf. Pat told us that the Buddhist name given to Shamara was also – Shamar Rinpoche's own sister's name; Karma Chime Donma; the Immortal Torch.

CHAPTER FOUR

FORTY-EIGHT DAYS

The days that followed were quiet. Melanie and I do not invite many guests to our home during the first days when one of our children is getting used to being in the world. Melanie needed to rest and I stayed home to prepare meals and look after Kai and Tina.

Every morning when we awoke, these two little girls would scramble into our room to look at and fondle their new sister. There was such pride and joy in their faces when Melanie would allow one of them to hold Shamara. They obediently went to school each morning, but upon returning home it was obvious that their hearts and minds had been with Shamara the whole time.

Our friends could not constrain themselves forever and flowers and cards soon began to arrive. But only a few people actually came by. Partly it was because of the weather. But it also seemed that our usually busy house was cloaked in a shroud that let only a few close friends in. What we later learned was that those who did come had first impressions of Shamara that were very much in keeping with her demeanor. She was a quiet, pensive child. She didn't coo, chortle or cry very much as one would have expected from an infant. Of course, when she was hungry she cried, but not in a very insistent way. During her waking hours, she seemed content just to look around. She would fuss if she was held too long and seemed most content when simply left alone. Her worst time of day was just before bed. She seemed to have more difficulty settling down at that time of the early evening than either Kai or Tina had had at her age. Yet, rocking or nursing her brought little comfort and she usually drifted off more easily when we simply left her alone in her cot.

One friend remarked that when she came to visit, she somehow felt that treating Shamara as an infant was not appropriate. In fact, she said that in Shamara's presence she wanted to kneel in respect. It was an odd remark to make but Melanie and I completely understood her sentiment.

My interaction with Kai and Tina as tiny babies had been very different from my interaction with Shamara. I had held and talked to both of them quite a lot. The emotional bonds were very warm. I was their Dad and it felt good. But with Shamara, I almost felt that such behavior was not what she was asking from me. When I held her, it was as though she wanted me to simply be silently present. Her eyes had a haunting quality about them. In the first few weeks, as a newborn baby takes in the world, any appearance of a direct visual focus on anyone or anything is simply accidental. Within a month, however, the baby's gaze generally becomes more direct and the contact more tangibly human. However, in the 48 days of Shamara's life we have no memories or photographs which would indicate that she ever made that shift in perception.

Probably the most meaningful contact I had with Shamara was within the context of meditation practice. I found myself reciting certain mantras to her: those of Loving Eyes (Chenrezig), the Bodhisattva of Compassion (probably the most famous mantra known in the west: OM MA NEE PEH MEH HOONG – as the Tibetans would say it) and of the Karmapa.

When I arose early in the morning she would stir. But, rather than demanding to be nursed, she was content for me to carry her into the shrine room where, often for the next hour and one half, she would gaze wide-eyed at our shrine. The noise of the bell and damaru (skull bone drum) which can be jarring to the senses when unfamiliar or unexpected never seemed to startle her. Being with Shamara in these times was like being with a close member of sangha (the name for Buddhist community), a fellow meditator. When Shamara began to get distracted, often toward the end of whatever meditation I was doing, Melanie - who was most appreciative of the additional rest - would come to get her for her morning nursing and bath.

The Dharma teaches about precious human birth and about impermanence. It teaches that while we can have the perfect physical and environmental conditions for practice and spiritual transformation, that this opportunity is both rare and fragile as a bubble. Indeed, when tending to children, you are aware of their vulnerability and how much they need your love and care to keep them safe and ensure that their needs are met.

But, whilst one is taught to be aware of the impermanence of it all and that life could end at any moment for any of us, it does not necessarily follow that – as a parent – you dwell or spend much time thinking that your baby will die. However, in our case, even though both our midwives and Walt reported to us how healthy and strong Shamara was at checkups, each morning we were amazed that she was actually still alive. And no matter how irrational and unlikely the thought and feelings seemed to us, it was impossible to rid ourselves of morbid thoughts. Still, in this time, I did not know that Melanie was thinking this way. Neither did she know that the same was happening for me.

The only incident that stands out most as a reflection of our state of mind occurred at Christmas. Being English, Melanie has always enjoyed preparing a traditional English-style Christmas event; from tree to stockings, traditional songs to a mid-day Christmas dinner. All of us were feeling festive throughout the morning as stockings were emptied of their treats and presents were opened. However, this mood changed when it came time to prepare the dinner.

Dinner was traditionally roast turkey with stuffing, potatoes and the like. On Christmas morning, Melanie began to have and express anxiety about preparing the turkey. Finally she openly confessed that handling it felt like handling a dead child. It was so unbearable that she could not even walk into the kitchen where it was resting on the counter. Yet, because we had traditionally celebrated the day in this manner and did not want to disappoint the children, we tried to blank out the tormenting thoughts and carry on.

So, on that Christmas day, I prepared the turkey. Eating it later on felt almost sacrilegious.

CHAPTER FIVE

OLE COMES TO VISIT

It was on January 16, 1983, on the 47th day of Shamara's life that our good friend Ole Nydahl came for a visit.

I first met Ole in April of 1975 when he was driving the great Kagyu Yogi, Kalu Rinpoche, through Europe. I was taking a break from my counseling training and had gone back to Kagyu Samye Ling Tibetan Centre in Eskdalemuir, Scotland for a short retreat. What seemed odd to me at that time was that virtually everyone I had previously met at Samye Ling was there all at one time. Initially I thought that everyone had taken up residence and that I was the only one really returning for a visit; not exactly clear logic. Soon enough I found out that most of these friends had returned for the same reason - to see Kalu Rinpoche.

Although the story of my taking Refuge into the Buddhist tradition with Kalu Rinpoche at this time has its own flavor of magic, I focus here on my interactions with the wild Dane, Ole, and his band of traveling Dharma warriors.

My first direct encounter with Ole was in the Samye Ling dining room. Dharma centers can be quite serious and sometimes even sanctimonious. And meal times at Samye Ling were no exception. People sat at benches eating in reflective states of mind - except for all of these Danes and Germans who beamed health and joy as they joked with each other.

I have learned over the years that such a joyous demeanor is one of the fruits of meditation practice. And much of this natural expression of joy is encouraged by Ole, who, as it happened, passed directly behind me as I sat appreciating my brown rice and vegetables. He stopped, placed both his hands on my shoulders and pressed his thumbs deep into my trapezius muscles with a fair amount of force. For whatever reason, I made no remark, nor did I flinch, even though I did feel a fair amount of pain as he kept his thumbs pressed in. When that magical, eternal moment had passed and he released the pressure, his only comment was, "Hmm. Not bad." No more was said and aside from a class where he gave the visualization on the Bodhisattva of Compassion, Chenrezig, I had no further interaction with Ole while at Samye Ling.

Four weeks later, Kalu Rinpoche was performing a ceremony, an empowerment on the Bodhisattva of Compassion, Chenrezig, at the Quaker Meeting House in central London. Perhaps 300 people came that night. As I had experienced at Samye Ling, the evening with Kalu Rinpoche was both intense and wonderful. It was especially so for me because while at Samye Ling, Kalu Rinpoche had given me refuge, the formal event where one consciously asks for and receives the blessing to become a Buddhist practitioner. He was my refuge lama. With good feelings and after a meaningful empowerment, I decided to leave the hall as people milled around and purchased prayer beads and incense from the vendors who are always at such events.

The hallways of the Quaker Meeting House are quite long and when you walk along them alone, the echo of your footsteps resounds. It was perhaps three-quarters down the hall that I began to hear the sound of running coming from behind. Not thinking that it had anything to do with me, I continued towards the door when, suddenly, a familiar hand was on my shoulder turning me around. I came face to face with Ole, who was already in the process of tying a red plastic protection cord around my neck. Looking into my eyes, he only said, "We'll meet again in the future." Somewhat dazed and obviously more confused than he, all I could say was, "If you say so."

Five years later in Woodstock, New York when His Holiness Karmapa was visiting, we had our reunion. We were like brothers who had not seen each other for years. There was an immediate recognition and sense of celebration between us. And that is how it has been since 1980. Wherever Melanie and I have lived, once and sometimes twice a year Ole has traveled there, bringing an ever increasing entourage of Dharma students from Europe, teaching, conferring blessings and then moving off again in the middle of the night to continue his ritual journeying across America to do what he is best at doing - inspiring friends and strangers alike to awaken to the nature of their own minds, the sole purpose of Buddhist Dharma.

Over the years and because of our connection through His Holiness, I had grown more and more perceptive as to when Ole was nearing where we lived. This certainly didn't have to do with agreed upon or approximate times of arrival. Ole travels in the fast lane. Sometimes he would leave one place at 1 a.m. after a teaching; sometimes the next day, after he and his friends have perused all the available thrift and army-navy stores in a region. Regardless, even if he arrives breathless, he has never been late for a teaching engagement. His arrival on January 16th was no different.

As had become my custom since Shamara's birth, I awoke early and took her upstairs with me to do my practice. Midway through our time in the shrine room, I felt a familiar feeling; the feeling that let me know that Ole was in the vicinity of Lexington. And, as usual, it was within moments of completing my practice that the phone rang. It was Ole, letting me know that he had stopped on the outskirts of Lexington with his friends to get some breakfast after an all-night drive from New York.

While it was still early morning hours, Melanie was soon up, as were Kai and Tina. And by about 6:30 a.m. Ole had arrived with his band of Danes and Germans. What Melanie and I noticed most about this particular group was that - as they came one at a time over the threshold of our front door - each traveler was taller than the preceding one. Even Ole's travel companion, Edita, seemed like a giant. And the largest was Burkhardt - indeed a gentle giant to whom our daughter Tina was immediately drawn. All of the travelers needed to rest. Some were to stay with us while others would stay with friends.

Besides all the comings and goings of people wanting to see Ole, a friend and psychic, John Kane, had arranged for Ole to be his guest on a local talk radio program in nearby Nicholasville, Kentucky. John was usually unaccompanied as he provided his psychic services to callers. He now had the added energy of Ole being broadcast into the Kentucky hills. Ole performed divinations for callers and answered their questions with a candor and directness that - without a doubt - shocked some of John's listening audience. I remember one caller who asked about an illness she was having and Ole suggested she visualize a blue Buddha in front of her - the Medicine Buddha. I will never forget how - in her thick Kentuckiana accent - she repeated, "Right, I visualize a blue Buddha."

Evening came around quickly. Our friends Ann Frye and Dick Levine had arranged for Ole to speak at the university. While I prepared sound equipment, cushions and the various bits and pieces needed for the evening, Melanie bathed Shamara with the help of Edita. Edita had grown particularly close to Shamara throughout the day and looked softened by having the opportunity to help one so young. Kai and Tina were to stay with friends while the rest of us went off to the talk.

The topic was the Four Noble Truths as taught by the Buddha. And one of Ole's greatest gifts is to be able to articulate such profound teachings in a way that touches people in their everyday experience of life. This is precisely what he did that evening with clarity, gentleness and humor.

It is one of those rare circumstances when both parents of an infant can sit together in a public event with the infant present and not find at least one of them tending to whatever needs arise. Shamara sat quietly for almost all of Ole's presentation. It was only towards the end, when he had opened up the talk to questions from the audience that Shamara became noticeably agitated and began to cry.

As she had not been nursed in a while, Melanie decided to leave the room and see if she could settle her. But Shamara persisted in crying and seemed inconsolable. More than half an hour went by and her crying remained unchanged. After Ole finished his presentation and we were closing up the room, we came out into the hallway to find Melanie still wearily pacing back and forth with Shamara.

Down in the parking lot, in the car, all the way home, Shamara's tears continued relentlessly and Melanie's anxiety and tension heightened. By the time we arrived home, Melanie was nearly beside herself. In such times - although they had never been so extreme - we would gently bundle Shamara up, lay her in her carry cot and place her in our shrine room. This always quieted her down faster than anything else and if she awakened, we could easily hear her from our bedroom. Tonight was no exception as once Melanie set Shamara in the shrine room, her tears subsided. Soon she was quiet. And for the first time in nearly 90 minutes, Melanie and I could sit down and spend time with Ole and our friends.

By 1:30 in the morning all of us had become sufficiently tired to get to sleep. There had not been

a sound from upstairs and rather than tempt fate,
Melanie just listened from the doorway instead of
going up the stairs to check on Shamara. As any parent
of a newborn baby knows, that first full night of sleep
after the baby is born is an eagerly awaited pleasure.
It seemed that tonight might be the night. Heavy
with tiredness and having no thought that anything
untoward was taking place, we went to bed. And the
night became still.

CHAPTER SIX

DEATH AND REBIRTH

Although I had gotten to bed later than usual, I still found myself awake at my regular hour.

Though I had slept deeply, just before rising I had a dream that so disturbed me that I felt as if all of the hairs on my body had been standing on end during the dream.

In the dream I was lying on my back in bed. Toward me, from the side door of the bedroom, walked a toothless, middle-aged hag with long black hair. Her mouth was twisted open to one side and she was dressed in a red T-shirt with Tibetan calligraphy on the front. She swayed as she walked and her cackle was blood curdling. The air around her was deathly cold. She came closer and closer until, finally, she was leaning over me, still cackling. And it was while looking up at her that I literally shook myself from sleep.

At that moment I made no real effort to determine the significance of the dream. It was morning and what seemed most significant was that Melanie and I had had our first full - albeit short - night's rest since Shamara's birth. After washing, I made my way up to the shrine room where Shamara's cot was. She was lying very still, face down in her cot. Even though she often slept like this, I found myself experiencing a pang of apprehension. I felt the back of her neck with the back of my hand. It was warm to my touch. And, oddly enough, I was surprised. I dismissed my feeling of apprehension. After all, had not both Melanie and I been dealing with such feelings almost every day of Shamara's life?

Thinking that I mustn't wake her too soon (lest I catch the wrath of a peacefully sleeping mother), I picked up Shamara's cot and moved it downstairs to the kitchen, where I assumed that once she stirred, Melanie would hear her and come to tend to her needs.

I began my morning meditation practice as usual, yet, at the same time, remained hyper-attentive as I waited for the sounds of Melanie rousing and coming to Shamara. I noted within myself how each moment was vivid and full - the way I usually get when something powerful is about to happen in my life.

Meanwhile, with the initial sounds of my meditation bells, Melanie awakened. As she lay there in bed, rather than savoring the feeling of being well-rested, her mind immediately went to thoughts of whether or not Shamara was alive. Both of us had dealt with these thoughts again and again; had put them out of our minds again and again. This time, however, Melanie allowed herself to dwell on them - to take them even further. What would she do if she found Shamara dead? First off, she thought, she would call our friend Gary Heinz, who was a carpenter. She would ask Gary to make a small pine coffin for Shamara. Who else would need to be contacted?

In order to shake herself free from these morbid thoughts, Melanie decided to get up and come to the shrine room to get Shamara. As she walked to the kitchen to open the door to the shrine room, she caught sight of Shamara's carry cot near the washing machine. Melanie was relieved with the thought that I had obviously checked Shamara to see that she was alright. Why else would I have brought her cot down to the kitchen?

I heard Melanie moving about downstairs and I was relieved, knowing that she was now with Shamara. And as quickly as that relief arose it was shattered with the sounds of Melanie's screams - screams which in an instant made me totally aware of what had happened.

I leaped down the stairs to find Melanie, half crouching, stiff, holding Shamara in her arms and screaming "Something is wrong!" I grabbed Shamara. She was stiff and cold and as I turned her over I saw that the whole left side of her face was blue and compressed. Mucous had hardened below her nose and on her upper lip and her mouth was twisted open - just like the hag in my dream.

It was obvious that she was dead. Yet somehow, Melanie and I wanted to deny the truth of what we were seeing. There was a feeling of total impotence. And, it was in that state of mental anguish and confusion that I ran with Shamara in my arms to Ole's room and burst in the door.

Ole met me right at the door. He had gotten up and was coming to us after hearing Melanie's screams. Holding Shamara's stiff body out to him, shaking, I shouted, "Do something!" Without a moment's hesitation and with a commanding directness he looked at me, took Shamara and said, "All right." He then went upstairs to the shrine room, sat down in front of the altar, placed Shamara upright on his lap and began the prayers for Phowa.

In the Tibetan Buddhist tradition, it is important to do spiritual practice during one's life for several reasons. First and foremost, by creating positive impressions in our minds through prayer and meditation focused with altruistic intentions, we become more open, dynamic and creative. Compassion toward others naturally arises. The second reason practice is so important is that it creates the seeds for a more positive rebirth by helping us to die more consciously. Phowa is a traditional practice that is particularly useful at the time of dying. Although it was primarily taught in a retreat setting as one of several practices to master while doing intense meditation, lamas would also teach it to lay persons who requested it. For the purpose of phowa is quite practical anyone. If in your spiritual journey there are still gaps in your education or experience, the yogic practice of phowa helps you exit your body at the time of death in the most auspicious manner possible. This happens spontaneously, almost reflexively, if you have been practicing the phowa method during your lifetime. Ones consciousness is born into a Buddha realm where, without any interference, one can continue your spiritual awakening. And once realization or enlightenment is firmly established, one can then consciously manifest in whatever realm of existence that seems most beneficial to help others still caught in suffering.

In Phowa, the meditator visualizes his or her body in a certain way and focuses attention on energies moving in the body. Through concentration, visualization and primordial sounds, this energy is gathered, concentrated, focused, aimed and shot out of the body through the psychic aperture in the crown of the head. (This is the area called the "soft spot" on a young child or the crown chakra in Eastern spiritual traditions.) This is important because the crown chakra is the doorway or conduit through which spiritual energy enters and can leave one's being if properly prepared. If one is able to do this through fortunate karma or the fortune of knowing the yoga of phowa, the best possible rebirth is ensured. In the Kagyu lineage that we practice, this means for ones consciousness to be propelled into the heart of the Amitabha Buddha and thus be born into his Pure Land, known as Dewachen.

When someone who has never learned the Phowa practice is dying or has just died, someone who is adept at this practice and understands how to do it for others is asked to perform the practice on the dying person's behalf. The reason this is possible is that the psychic energy in the body does not leave immediately. Initially what happens is that, as the elements of the body dissolve, the psychic energy moves towards the heart. As long as there is heat around the heart of the deceased, the psychic force is still present.

The length of time this heat remains depends upon the individual's spiritual development. If there is little development, the heat may leave within a few hours. For the average person it takes about three days, which is probably why so many indigenous cultures

composure to give us professional advice as to what steps we would need to take. The first thing I needed to do was to get in touch with the coroner's office.

Within a half-hour of calling, the deputy coroner arrived. He was a young, graceful man with a moustache. He was well-trained at being the bearer of bad tidings. He demonstrated a natural, gentle quality of empathy as he entered the house. Of course, he wanted to see Shamara and I had to explain to him in some way what basically was going on upstairs. I led him upstairs and he remained for a few minutes while Ole continued the Phowa. He then came downstairs and sat, saying that he would wait for the ceremony to end. In the meantime, he called the police photographer who arrived shortly thereafter.

In this time, I also made a call to Karma Triyana Dharmachakra, where I presumed my teacher, Khenpo Karthar Rinpoche was. The secretary told me that Khenpo Rinpoche was in New York City and that I would have to call him at the meditation center there. When I made that call I learned that, in fact, Rinpoche was not at the center but somewhere in the city, so I left a message of what had happened.

From the time Ole began Phowa and I started through the ordeal of telling our daughters, Walt, the deputy coroner and the police photographer and trying to contact Khenpo Rinpoche, a little over an hour passed. There was a feeling of chaotic heaviness that made each moment seem eternal. This atmosphere was broken as Ole called Melanie and me upstairs in what sounded like a completely joyful tone of voice.

He had placed Shamara on her back in her little carry-cot and both Melanie and I looked at her in amazement. The blueness had left her face, her mouth was normal and her appearance peaceful, almost radiant. And, from her nose there was streaming a clear fluid. This fluid had been preceded by a long strand of white foam which Ole and Edita watched being literally propelled out of her nose at the moment when Ole had felt the transference of Shamara's consciousness taking place. Although Melanie and I did not witness this, just knowing how Shamara had looked when we found her and seeing her now after Phowa was convincing enough. Something remarkable and unexplainable in any medical or scientific terms had happened to her in less than an hour. The phowa had transformed her and if the goal of this practice was to be reborn in Dewachen, regardless of whether Melanie or I would know this with any certainty or not, we were quite prepared to accept this as truth. We were witnessing miracles in the moment. The world was changing before our eyes. And the phowa was introducing us to Amitabha's Pure Land.

In the mix of emotions, of pain, sorrow, and joy, we were just beginning to grasp. It would have been easy to remain transfixed by the miracle. However, we were compelled to deal with other mundane but necessary issues.

We called for the deputy coroner to come up to the shrine room. He was completely astounded since, just half an hour before, he had seen Shamara's cold, blue, distorted appearance. The photographer also came upstairs, but, since he did not realize what had happened, he simply took her photos and departed. When both of them went downstairs, we called Tina and Kai. With tears in their eyes and acting very bravely, they came upstairs to say good-bye to Shamara. Ever so delicately, they each kissed her cheek. Edita and Burkhardt then held their hands and led them downstairs. Ole produced a relic from the great Kumboom stupa and placed it in the bonnet that Shamara still wore. I went downstairs to get the red T-shirt with Tibetan calligraphy that I had gotten the last time I was in New York. It was the same one that the hag had worn in my dream. It was Shamara's and I wanted her to be cremated with it.

Ole told us that the deputy coroner could take Shamara's body - that it was now an empty vessel. I was still in disbelief of what had happened and admittedly was not as certain of Ole's ability in phowa as I now am. I wanted Khenpo Rinpoche to say that it was all right to let her go.

This time when I called, Tenzin Chonyi, president of the monastery and then one of the translators for Khenpo Rinpoche answered the phone. With his clairvoyant-like abilities, Rinpoche was able to confirm that the transference of consciousness had occurred for Shamara. Rinpoche and Ole then talked for a few minutes about what had happened. Melanie then got on the phone with Tenzin who spoke in a most understanding way. He told Melanie that normally he does not remember dreams but, that night, the night Shamara had passed, he had a dream that a small child was reborn into Amitabha's Pure Land.

With Tenzin and Rinpoche's words I now felt prepared to let the deputy coroner take Shamara. Still wrapped in her night clothes and bonnet, with a piece of a Buddhist shrine placed above the crown of her head by Lama Ole and wearing a red T-shirt with the Tibetan tantric OM symbol at the heart, the deputy carried Shamara's cot to the car and drove off. We waved good-bye from the porch. Later on we heard from the deputy coroner. The coroner's report was that the autopsy revealed that Shamara had been in excellent health. It was also evident that she had been well cared for. His diagnosis was that she had died of Sudden infant Death Syndrome; SIDS.

Birth and - we now learned - death are primordial events. They occur all the time, yet they are extraordinary in how they make it effortless to drop what is superfluous from one's life and make one focus in the here and now of what truly needs to be done. No doubt such attention and action is facilitated by the blanket of shock that one is physically and psychically experiencing at such times.

Kai and Tina needed baths. Edita and Burkhardt tended to them. Melanie and I called our respective parents. Melanie's parents, being in Britain, could only grieve with us from a distance. My parents, from whom I had been estranged for some time, responded immediately by saying that they were on their way from Florida to be with us. The house needed to be cleaned. We were still in the middle of Ole's visit. People would be calling for appointments.

Then there was the fact that we had made a public announcement about a talk by Ole at our house that night. Not knowing who would come, we decided to let it all happen. And, we were hungry.

I had been told by others that death can make one hungry. And no doubt for all of us, that was true as we seemed to eat an enormous volume of food at a hotel all-you-can-eat salad bar. It did not feel like we were eating to hold down feelings. In fact, life felt so vivid, so clear. There was a tremendous sense of caring among all of us there; Ole, Edita, Burkhardt, other German friends, Melanie, myself, Kai and Tina. And it was in this state of mind that Ole told us a story about another little girl that he knew.

An American couple had given birth to a little girl a few years before. When she turned two years of age, her parents decided that they wanted to take her with them on a trip to Thailand to see Southeast Asia, especially the great Thai Buddhist temples.

Once they had toured Thailand and other parts of Southeast Asia, they decided to go to Sikkim to see their teacher, the Sixteenth Karmapa. They had been at Rumtek, the monastery of the Karmapa, just one night when, during the night, their daughter died.

This was clearly not a case of SIDS as SIDS is medically considered to occur only to children less than one year of age. Totally beside themselves with grief they went to the Karmapa to ask him what had gone wrong.

The Karmapa looked at them and smiled. He told them that nothing had gone wrong. Still they wanted a reason. And so he gave them one. His

Holiness had known their daughter in her previous life. She had been a very famous religious adept, a yogini. When she was dying, she apparently told His Holiness that in her next life all she wanted to do was see a few of the great temples of Thailand and that would be enough. In this lifetime, her parents fulfilled her request. And she could then leave.

Our own daughter was born into an atmosphere still charged with the blessing of our teacher, Khenpo Karthar Rinpoche. She heard mantras at birth and heard prayers daily. Her last night alive was at a Dharma talk. And, she died in the presence of a lama and phowa Master.

Years later I learned the significance of my dream of the hag. A Tibetan doctor and monk explained that a hag in a dream signifies that life is being taken away to another place - a reminder that life goes on and that death is the shroud it must don in order to move from one place to the next. In Shamara's case, a Pure Land.

CHAPTER SEVEN

TEN DAYS OF MIRACLES

I have learned over the years from my conversation with others who have been in the presence of death, that they witnessed omens and signs before and after the time of dying. For these people such occurrences were miraculous and transformative. In actual fact, I believe such occurrences are normal; they happen all the time. It is just a matter of how awake one is at the time they take place. It seems that life is constantly giving us opportunities to wake up, become conscious - to see clearly what is and is not important in the course of our lives.

Having said that, let me also say that I do not consider myself to be very awake at all. However, the events that took place over the next 10 days after Shamara's passing were so blatant that Melanie and I would have to have been comatose not to see them as miracles and opportunities to awaken to a deeper level of spiritual reality.

After returning home from lunch at the hotel, there were more mundane affairs to be tended to. There was still going to be a talk by Ole at our home that evening. We had to clean and prepare for whoever would appear at our door. By this time, the morning's occurrences had been passed on via the community grapevine. We knew that some of our friends would be coming, almost as if to a funeral service. There would also be others who were not aware of what

had happened and were simply expecting to come
to a special Dharma talk. And there were Melanie,
the children and myself; tired, in shock, in pain and
strangely filled with joy at knowing what had taken
place for Shamara.

The talk was at 7:30 and people began to arrive
at 7:00. It was obvious from facial expressions who
knew and who didn't. Death is not a word that we
like to use in social settings. So to those who were not
aware of what had happened, it must have seemed
bizarre to see others come in tearful, sad, wanting to
give hugs and be close.

It was actually rather strange. Both Melanie
and I felt that much of what we needed to do was
to comfort these people. They were seemingly here
for us, but on a deeper level, Shamara's passing had
evoked deep feelings and questions in all of them.

When 7:30 came around and everyone was
gathered upstairs in the shrine room, Ole, Melanie
and I went up and sat in front of what must have been
50 people.

I had told people that the talk for the evening
was going to be different than what we had advertised.
It was going to be about death, impermanence and the
importance of Dharma practice in our lives. And I told
them why we had changed the program.

A visible shudder went through the room as my
words telling them about Shamara's passing sank in.
Everyone's breathing became deeper. And while some
eyes filled with tears, others simply stared forward
in discomfort - as if something were being evoked
for which they were not prepared. In the presence

of the energy of phowa, so much love was present
that it seemed as if each friend were being honored
by whatever he or she was experiencing in those
moments. And in that atmosphere, Ole began his talk
which was both moving and direct in its message. We
all became engulfed in the sacredness of the moment.

Ole always does a meditation at the end of his
talks and on this evening, he gave the visualization
one of the previous incarnations of the Karmapa
lama, Mikyo Dorje. Ole has mastered the timing and
presentation of guided meditations and his voice
seemed to create an atmosphere of blessing energy
flowing down from the Karmapa he encouraged us
all to visualize. He told us imagine that this blessing
appeared as snowflakes descending around us and
filling our entire bodies.

The warmth and caring we all felt in that room
made it seem as if we could remain there forever. Any
thought of parting for the evening seemed unreal.
As people came down from the shrine room, many
came to Melanie and me. So many of them had been
deeply touched by the evening, so much so that one
friend, who had recently had an abortion, told us that
if she ever got pregnant again, knowing how uncertain
the course of life is, that she would definitely keep
the child and do her best to bring it into the world.
Another group of friends had gotten together to
give us some money so that Melanie and I could take
some time off work. Our friend and midwife, Noni,
returned our check for her services as midwife in
Shamara's birth. Though Melanie protested, Noni was
so earnestly insistent that we accepted. Ironically the

amount Noni returned to us was exactly the cost for Shamara's cremation. Another friend had the unusual request of wanting Melanie to express breast milk for a niece of hers who was dying of leukemia. Melanie obliged.

Many other friends told us that they would be in touch with us to help out in any way that they could. So many friends we had made in Lexington. And in true friendship, it seemed, they were opening their hearts to us. Evenings with Ole always run late and, finally, everyone was gone and the house was quiet. The night was clear and mild.

Morning came around silently - a new experience as both Melanie and I had gotten used to Shamara's stirrings. It was a reminder to us that the passing had not been a dream.

The light of dawn was just appearing. As I passed the dining room windows, I looked out to find the entire neighborhood covered in a velvet blanket of pure white snow. This was such a contrast to what the weather of the previous days and even the night before had been. And, in an instant, I recalled Ole's meditation on the blessing of Mikyo Dorje descending upon us like flakes of snow. My heart was comforted by seeing nature in synchronicity with sacred vision and our aspirations. In such a state of mind I went up to the shrine room.

Normally I would have emptied the offering bowls I place on the shrine every morning before going to sleep. I had been just too tired to be bothered with it so late the night before. Thus I was aware that

I needed to empty the bowls and prepare them anew before beginning my meditation practice for the day.

I was not prepared for what I saw.

Many of the bowls of water were almost empty, still upright. Food offerings that had been on the shrine were not there or just small amounts were remaining. Being the last one in the shrine room for the night, I was totally certain that no one visiting from the night before had gone and helped themselves to these offerings, something almost preposterous to consider anyways. And, we had no mice that I was aware of and it wasn't hot enough for the amount of water that was missing from the water offerings to have evaporated. Therefore, my mind came around to what seemed a possible but somewhat miraculous conclusion: that beings from other levels of existence that are identified in Buddhist practice, known as dakinis and other deities to whom Buddhists make such offerings, had actually come and accepted our offering to them!

Being in an atmosphere that was evidently saturated with blessing and in a state where solid reality was quite obviously being transformed in our minds, I was at once joyful and amazed, yet at the same time, quite calm and accepting of such manifestations. Ole, Melanie, Edita and others had similar reactions.

It was soon after practice that friends began to call. Some had talked the night before about wanting to learn more about Phowa. Others were calling now for the same reason. I spoke with Ole and he agreed to get together with all those interested to teach the visualization for Phowa. And at 11 a.m. the morning of January 18th, Ole taught the visualization for Phowa for the first time in the United States. This was to be the first of many gatherings where Ole has fulfilled the wishes of his teacher, the Venerable Tenga Rinpoche, to teach Phowa in the West.

Melanie and I were almost in a state of suspended animation for the next few days. And Ole, Edita and Burkhardt stayed with us as friends and guides. They were joined by Geoff and Diana who had grown keenly aware of what Khenpo Rinpoche had requested of them only eight weeks ago. It was they, in fact, who kept our daily lives together, helping us with meals, sorting out mail and doing whatever was needed to keep ordinary life moving forward. Kai and Tina went back to school, but we allowed them to come home any time if they felt shaky or just wanted to stay close to us.

It was on January 20th in the morning that Ole departed with Edita, Burkhardt and a few of the others in the entourage who had stayed on in Lexington for those few days. We had grown close to each one of them and over the years our reunions with them have been filled with a special warmth and appreciation. As for Ole, our love and appreciation for his commitment to the Karmapa and the Dharma and what he had done for Shamara made our connection to him diamond-like; indestructible.

Soon after Ole and our European friends departed Lexington, my parents arrived from Florida. It is not unusual for death to bring a family closer together. Issues of attitude and lifestyle which might

have generated heated discussion at other times seem
petty in the face of death. Thus it was the vitriol that
had been so much a part of the relationship that
Melanie and I had with my parents over the last two
years dropped away in the wake of what most families
would consider a tragedy and a much needed and
welcome healing process between us began.

What seemed to bring this about most was my
mother's and father's observation of how Melanie and
I were handling ourselves and Kai and Tina. Because
we had received so many concerned calls and visits
from friends, I decided to make a tape recording
of the events that took place and how Melanie and
I viewed them so that we would not have to repeat
ourselves constantly. Months later my mother was to
comment that letting them listen to that tape helped
them a great deal in understanding us as well as the
practice of Buddhism.

My mother helped watch Kai and Tina and
my father, in his characteristic way, remained a
silent, powerful support. It was he who drove us to
the coroner's office to pick up Shamara's ashes. It
felt eerie to be holding a plastic container with the
cremated remains of the tiny baby we had held in our
arms only days before.

We had already decided to mail the ashes
to Shamar Rinpoche in India. Ole had said that it
was traditional for lamas to be given the ashes of
the deceased. They would dispose of or use them in
ceremonial ways and this seemed the most fitting
use for Shamara's ashes. The trip to the post office,
mailing the package, driving home - all were done in

a dream-like state. My father's love and care in those hours held a warmth that nurtured both Melanie and me.

I had not yet returned to work. And the calls kept coming in as did flowers, cards, food and whatever forms of care and support friends could offer. But what was also apparent to us was how much pain everyone around us was in. It was almost more overwhelming than our own feelings. Too often we found ourselves in the role of offering time for consolation. Thus it was that after talking with my parents and Geoff and Diana, it seemed that the best thing for us would be to go away for a while. Melanie and I decided to go to visit Khenpo Rinpoche in Woodstock, New York.

The day Melanie, Kai, Tina and I left Lexington was overcast and cold. The energy and blessing of the time around Shamara's transference seemed to fade into the darkness of our sense of loss. The weather accurately reflected our mood. Fifteen miles north of Lexington I was stopped for speeding. Normally I would have chatted with the officer in the hopes that my friendliness would let us get off with a warning. But I couldn't be bothered. As if the ticket were just part of what the darkness was offering, I accepted it and drove off.

We had decided that Kai and Tina would be better served by staying with our dear friends, Charles and Deborah Dawes and their three children, Daniel, Jonathan and Rosemary. We had been friends in the Columbus, Ohio Buddhist community and our children were of similar ages. Kai and Tina liked the idea as did the Dawes family. We only spent a short time getting the children settled in before Melanie and I were on our way to Woodstock.

This was an unusual situation for Melanie and me - for there to be just the two of us, alone and on the road. It was a relief not to have to relate to anyone else. We did not speak very much. Occasionally we just held hands. Silence and touch were all that was needed.

By our calculations, it would be midnight by the time we got to the monastery. Rinpoche was happy we were coming and Ngodrup Burkhar had let Tenzin Chonyi know that as he, Marianne and their daughter, Kalsang, were out of town that Melanie and I could use their cabin for the duration of our stay. It was a short distance from the monastery's main building. The privacy would be most welcome.

As we traveled along Interstate 80 at dusk, it became more and more obvious with each mile that we were driving into a winter storm front. Small flakes of snow hitting the windshield became larger and more constant. Drifts swirled toward the car as the wind speed increased. I had been raised in Cleveland, so driving in such conditions was not unfamiliar. We pressed on.

By 11:30 p.m., with more and more ice on the road and travel speed greatly reduced, we knew that we would be much longer than anticipated. Both of us felt alert. There seemed to be no point in stopping; just go with things as they were. We were now traveling about 35 miles per hour along the freeway. Visibility was down to less than 10 feet. It was hard to know where the lanes were, since we could only use our low beam lights as the brights only intensified the glare off the snow.

Both Melanie and I were silent and focusing on the road. It was in that frame of mind that the silence was shattered by a large truck passing us on the right side, going at least double our speed. The size and speed of this truck blinded us with more snow and the tail wind made the car begin to swerve. And no sooner had this happened than on the left, another truck passed, going even faster.

The combined force of the tail winds and snow thrown by both trucks reduced our visibility to zero and made steering impossible. We were fish-tailing wildly down the road with each yard feeling like it would lead us into a total spin. Trying to brake and adjust my steering was not even a consideration. In that moment - where there seemed no choice - I let go of the wheel completely. Melanie and I braced ourselves for what seemed to be a fatal situation.

In the space of those moments sliding down the freeway out of control, a force like a large hand coming out of the sky seemed to grab the car. No sooner had Melanie and I felt this presence, than, for no apparent reason, the car began moving in a straight line down the road again. The steering wheel had stopped spinning. I was once again able to place my hands on it. And it was as if nothing unusual had happened.

We drove on for a few minutes until we saw arrows pointing to a roadside rest area. I pulled into a parking space and turned off the engine. And we just sat looking at each other. "What happened?" Melanie asked sheepishly. I certainly had no answer; at least no answer that would make sense in three-dimensional, linear, rational reality. Somehow, we both knew that a presence beyond our normal senses had just prevented us from dying in the middle of the night on the Pennsylvania thruway.

Later on, as we talked about what had happened in those few seconds, it seemed that we had both faced them in a similar mind state. It was as if a gap had appeared for us. We were totally open and in that open space, we had both silently chanted the mantra, "Karmapa Cheno." And since we had both silently and spontaneously chanted the mantra of Karmapa, we felt that it was his blessing that had made this miracle arise.

In that moment we took only a short time to reflect on our blessing. Even though the road was getting worse, even though we had just had a brush with death, the power of this event gave us the resolve to keep going - to get to our spiritual home and be with our spiritual father.

Darkness gave way to light as we drove on through the stormy night. Passing through the town of Woodstock in the early morning, we were virtually the only car on the road. Here, too, it was bleak, gray and stormy with roads covered in slush and ice. We decided to use the less steep, back road up to the monastery as we were concerned that the front road would be impassable.

As we wearily drove those last few miles up that road, we became enveloped in the same cloud cover which shrouded the mountain on whose crest the monastery is situated. It seemed that all the gray and the darkness of the preceding night was culminating on these slopes. Then, as if in a dream, as we approached the summit where Karma Triyana sits, the entire sky opened up before us. The clouds melted away, the sky was a deep blue and the monastery and snow covered land around it were vivid in the dazzling light. It was a glorious sight. Our 21 hour journey had come to an end. I parked the car and, with a sigh, we got out.

Morning meditation on the female Protectoress Green Tara was just finishing as Melanie and I sat, drinking a cup of tea in the monastery dining room. It wasn't but a few minutes till Khenpo Rinpoche walked in. Never straying from total awareness, he came in silently, seeming to not even disturb the particles of dust in the air. His gaze was one of pain and benevolence as he came toward us and embraced us one at a time. In his arms, Melanie was able to weep openly for the first time since Shamara's passing. Rinpoche indicated that we could get together with him in the afternoon. For now, we were to eat, settle in and rest.

The morning passed while Melanie and I rested. It felt as though we had not slept in weeks.

In the afternoon of that first day we met with Rinpoche and the translator, Tenzin. We talked with Rinpoche about the Phowa and expressed our interest in pursuing its study and practice. There were preliminary practices he wanted us to do to ensure that we would see the benefits of doing Phowa. He also gave us some protective visualizations to use in the practice, for if done improperly, one's life force can be dissipated rapidly while practicing Phowa.

He also told us in a tone that I have come to never question that what had happened to us with Shamara would not happen again were we to have another child. Here he was not addressing the miracle that had taken place, but the ordinary Melanie and me who felt the pain and loss.

Rinpoche's prayers are powerful and we felt a new strength enter us as he spoke and prayed over us. He then presented us with one of his personal shrine statues. It was of Green Tara, the protectoress who was formed from the tear of the great Bodhisattva, Chenrezig. To this day, she sits prominently on our altar. We make prayers to her.

In the warmth of the love Khenpo Rinpoche had shown us, the days that followed were uneventful, save that they were quite nurturing; sleeping without interruption, preparing simple meals in Ngodrup and Marianne's kitchen, meditating, taking walks to the Magic Meadow, visiting friends and helping with monastery chores as needed.

The weather had grown colder and more snow covered the mountain. Periodically we ventured into town; but by the 5th day, unless one had a truck or a four-wheel drive, leaving the monastery was neither practical nor safe. Looking back on this time, it has become apparent to both Melanie and me that invisible forces were once again at work. The cold and snow slowed us down, encouraged us to take time, to allow ourselves to be nurtured and to prepare for what was to come next. It was now 10 days since Shamara's passing.

On that 10th day, Melanie and I had reluctantly driven down to Woodstock for some items we needed. There had been a plan for us to have dinner with some friends in town, but they were cancelled at the last moment and it was actually a relief to be heading back to the quiet safety of the little cabin we had been living in. The snow was becoming heavier and we were happy to park the car for the day. As we left the car, we observed several friends coming in and out of the lama's house in a somewhat frantic state.

We were told by one friend, Flo, that Saima, another of the monastery residents, was about ready to give birth. She asked if I would be prepared to drive her to the hospital. Melanie and I did not know Saima, but doing that for her was no problem. Still, we wanted to meet Saima, to see how she was doing.

We entered into Saima's room in the basement of the lama's house. In her early 40s, she was a vibrant woman of Finnish extraction, very steely, yet soft and radiant at the same time. And she was very definitely in the latter stages of labor.

A call had been put through to her doctor. Saima wanted him to come to the monastery to birth the baby there, but he was insistent that she meet him at the hospital. Saima's labor had gone fast up to this point and she was not convinced that she would make it to the hospital on time with weather conditions as they were.

Her fear was compounded by the fact that her own mother had hemorrhaged and died when Saima was being delivered. The thought of being without medical support terrified her. She hoped that if she just held out, the doctor would see that there was no choice but to come. The problem was that with every passing minute, the roads leading to town became more and more treacherous. Melanie and I talked it over and it was decided that she would stay with Saima to help with the labor. Hopefully, one more call to the doctor would convince him to come to the monastery. In case it became clear that this wasn't going to happen and birth was imminent, Melanie would call me at Ngodrup's house to come get Saima in the car and take her to the hospital.

I decided to make myself useful by preparing the evening meal for Melanie and me. However, it wasn't even 20 minutes until I got the call. In that short time Melanie could see that Saima was going through transition. If she was going to be transported at all, it had to happen now. As a precaution, Flo had called the paramedic unit to come up to the monastery if we couldn't get out.

I dropped the back seat on our Pinto wagon, put a mattress inside to make Saima less uncomfortable and pulled around to the lama's house. Walking into the room where Saima was, however, made me change my mind about transporting her. I had been through three home births with Melanie and was very familiar with what a woman looks like when the baby is about to come.

In a moment of calm in the storm of contractions, I asked Saima if she would mind me checking her vaginally to see where the baby's head was. (In such times, modesty is not a primary consideration.) She consented and reaching in I found - not to my surprise - that the baby's head was crowning. "Saima," I said, "you're not going anywhere. We're going to do this right here and now."

While Melanie helped Saima relax her breathing, I massaged acupressure points to help prevent hemorrhaging and then massaged her perineum to encourage the tissues to stretch and allow the head through without tearing.

In birth, as in death, there is no awareness outside that of the present moment. Against the background of having given birth to a baby daughter just eight weeks ago and then of losing her to SIDS, our actions felt grounded in a way that made the intensity of the ordeal seem as ordinary as it was profound. Saima seemed reassured in our presence. Flo and Naomi looked on and provided support while Saima, Melanie and I got on with birthing the baby.

In less than 10 minutes, Karma Sherab Zangpo was born. When his head came out, I recited the mantra of Karmapa to him as I had done for Shamara. I had never assisted at the birth of a baby boy before. He was feisty. I laid him on Saima's belly. Once again I massaged points to prevent bleeding. Saima had not torn. There was minimal blood. She was fine. The baby was fine.

Later that night, in the silence of the cabin, Melanie and I reflected on Sherab Zangpo's birth. What struck us at the time was the similarity of the energy surrounding birth and death. Coming into life. Leaving life. Both are transitions. Entering the Bardo

of living in a body - beginning at the moment of birth.
And entering the Bardo of consciousness between lives
- beginning at the moment of death. We were learning
in possibly the most graphic way the truth of what in
Buddhism is called the Four Ordinary Foundations:
that life is precious; that it is as fragile as a bubble
and that one can die at any time; that the lives we
experience are the result of our own actions; and that
being preoccupied with anything other than spiritual
unfoldment is frivolous.

This very personal teaching in the moment
also pointed to a larger reality. Ten days earlier we
had witnessed the death of Shamara and her rebirth
into Amitabha's Pure Land. Miracle after miracle had
sharpened our senses. Our trip to Woodstock had felt
necessary. At the moment the idea came to us, we were
still caught up in the smaller picture of our own need
to get away. The larger necessity was that had Melanie
and I not been at the monastery 10 days later, we
would not have been able to bring Sherab Zangpo into
the world. In the bigger picture, there seemed to be a
connection between our daughter, named by one of
the teachers we venerate the most, and this little boy,
born of a Finnish mother and Tibetan father in the
lama's house at Karma Triyana Dharmachakra. Perhaps
Karma Sherab Zangpo is a reincarnate. Perhaps not.
We certainly are not ones to know. But, what we do
know and what seems to matter is that Melanie and I
were offered events of life and death, of miracles to
help us wake up to a more vast and sacred vision of the
world around us. It was our own rebirth into a Pure
Land - the Pure Land where all sights, sounds, visions

and experiences are none other than expressions of the awakened state of mind; of Buddha.

Of course, there are times where we catch ourselves napping, preoccupied in the mesmerizing web of conditioned three-dimensional reality; what in Buddhism is known as samsara. It is hard to awaken from our habitually reinforced hallucinations. It takes practice. But perhaps what makes it a little easier is when we reflect on the powerful, magical time when the pure practicality of the Dharma - the Buddha's teaching - was made transparently clear in our own lives.

In looking around me, I now see that these opportunities to wake up are always there. Buddha nature is not hiding itself. We just need to uncover our eyes and trust our hearts. Where we are, here and now, is indeed a Pure Land.

CHAPTER EIGHT

THE PASSAGE OF TIME

(Twenty-seven years after her passing, I decided to share with a wider audience Shamara's story. When I wrote this section of the first edition of this book some 20 years ago, I was thinking more parochially and not much beyond the small enclave of Buddhists who I thought might enjoy the tale. But, after many years of working as a hospice social worker and bereavement counselor, I now see more clearly how Shamara's story and the reflections and conclusions I have come to strike the universal chords to which we are all connected. Thus I have decided to include the reflections I made all those years ago with those that I have grown into over the last twenty years, including updates on some of the key figures of the time.)

Shamara's passing, her rebirth into Dewachen and other transforming events that have often felt linked to those days in the time of Shamara, have informed and guided Melanie and me in our choices of direction, our actions, and our views.

No matter how profound or sacred events may be, they cannot entirely counteract natural - or more accurately, habitual - human instincts and responses. It is not uncommon for couples to be so traumatized by SIDS that their own health deteriorates and they divorce. Returning from Woodstock, Melanie felt empty and purposeless, which led her into a depression. Within a year she was diagnosed with cervical cancer.

I am convinced that the blessing and power of what we experienced gave us the will and strength to face each other and for Melanie to choose life rather than death.

Melanie's direction in life and health was transformed in her meeting of Dr. Vasant Lad while we helped to run the kitchen at the Omega Institute in Rhinebeck, New York. His spirit and the precision and gentleness of Ayurvedic medicine touched her deeply. Within a year, through applying all of what we knew of health care, following Dr. Lad's instructions and cutting through her negative emotional patterns using meditation and self examination, she was free of cancer.

She then decided to begin a correspondence course with Dr. Lad through his Ayurvedic Institute in Albuquerque, New Mexico. Seven years later, after completing the correspondence course, a year-long program with Dr. Lad and applying what she studied in this discipline and the whole gamut of alternative health care practices we have made it our business to learn, Melanie published Ayurvedic Beauty Care, the consummate modern text on beauty care in Ayurveda. Today, she is the co-owner of our company, Diamond Way Ayurveda. Not only is she the leading international spokesperson on Ayurveda for the entire spa and beauty industries, she has also become the maker of extraordinary fairy beings who uplift and inspire those who feel the magic and grace that

Melanie puts into each of these small beings. She has also become a doting grandmother.

As for myself, when we returned to Lexington after our trip to Woodstock, I decided that I wanted further training and education and thus pursued a Masters in Social Work. It seemed the most effective means for me to be able to reach more people. I still pursued all of what Melanie and I had been learning in preventive health care. In these times, our friend Rex Lassalle stands out as an inspiration.

Seeing more potential in both Melanie and me than we saw in ourselves, Rex prodded and even financed us so that we could explore new directions and find new avenues into the greater alternative and spiritual communities in America and Europe. It is through his kindness that I became inspired to publish a book on Nine-Star Ki Astrology (called The Complete Guide To Nine-Star Ki) and study Tibetan Tai Chi. It was he who enabled both Melanie and me to receive all of the Kagyu Buddhist empowerments at the Kagyu Ngadzo in Denmark in 1989. Possibly because he had faced death himself, Rex was there for us in a time when what we had learned needed to be transformed into practical skills for living - and making a living.

Today, along with Melanie, I have been co-directing our company Diamond Way Ayurveda. After working in social work settings for chemical dependency and hospice, I find myself more like a Buddhist "rabbi," seeing people privately, doing Ayurvedic treatments, and writing. My books have covered any number of subjects that I thought it would be useful for me to put my mind and pen to; death and dying, Tibetan Ayurveda, relationships, and how to make Buddhist sensibility come alive in daily living. And over the years, the zealot quality of my Buddhist practice has subsided and been replaced with a more gentle and equanimitous approach. I think this is easier on everyone.

Seven years after Shamara's passing, Melanie and I gave birth to our son, Jabeth David-Francis. In Tibetan he is called Karma Jigme Dorje. It is ironic that he is most afraid of thunder when his name means "fearless thunderbolt." It is a name given to him by Khenpo Rinpoche who could see Jabeth before he was born. We do not know what his future holds for him, but he is a blessing to us. In his birth, confidence in the physical level of her being returned to Melanie. And for Kai and Tina, the light that went out of their eyes seven years earlier returned. They love and dearly care for their little brother in a way that lets us know that they, too, understand about precious human birth and impermanence. Jabeth is now 20 years of age. He is not sure what he wants to become, but his love, compassion, and the protector qualities he shows towards friends and everyone he meets is extraordinary. A freedom fighter, a lama, psychotherapist, or rock star. Whatever path he goes, we are proud of him and know that his heart is always in the right place. And, as for his sisters, Kai Ling is a mom and has our only grandchild, Braedon James. She is our protector child with a fierceness and brilliance that is only matched by her soft caring soul. She is training to become a health and physical education teacher. Christina graduated from college in fine arts and, after doing a variety of jobs that have trained her in managing others, she is looking at how art can serve community. She carries the twinkly dakini energy of Melanie's family and loves the fairy realm as much as her mother. It was a joy to take all three of them to a phowa course with Lama Ole in 2009 – the first time he has ever had three generations of one family come to receive phowa.

In the time of writing the first edition of this book, I made efforts to contact the many friends who were a part of what I venture to call Shamara's inner circle. In particular, I was able to find one of our midwife's, Noni Rhodes. Noni and her family had moved to Florida soon after we left Lexington. Yet, after participating in the birthing of so many more babies along the way, her time with Shamara is still so vivid in her mind. Honoring a request for her to offer a comment for this book, Noni wrote the following epitaph for Shamara.

Noni's Epitaph to Shamara

"Shamara was born softly, gently and welcomed in joyous ceremony by her family and friends. I was a privileged witness to the beauty and vitality of her tiny being. That Shamara would pass as softly and swiftly as morning showers did not occur to me. In my mind's eye I see her wise countenance peering out of her mother's warm coat, papoosed carefully into her infant "front pack." I smiled to see the mother and proud big sisters stroll our neighborhood on daily outings. She was cherished.

The effect of Shamara's passing was profound. Shock, grief, sadness, anger, bewilderment name but do not ex-press the tumultuous emotion which grips body and soul like a storm surfacing and resurfacing unbidden. Kai was best friends with my daughter, Kelly. I remember them talking and retelling the story of Shamara. Then the story stopped and silence took its place. Their play was punctuated by strong words of anger, unaccountably.

Making meaning from loss is the healing energy which propels us forward. It does not appear instantaneously, but evolves beginning with love (birth), loss of love (death - or so we feel at the time) resulting in anger, sadness and grief. Only in experiencing these can we move forward to meaning, greater strength and understanding. It is then that we say, 'I was privileged to know this remarkable soul.'"

Throughout the years, Khenpo Rinpoche remained our spiritual father and a third grandfather to our children. In formal practice and helping us in practical living circumstances, he has manifested to us all the actions of a Bodhisattva. As teacher and protector he is - in our eyes - impeccable and beyond reproach. We love him dearly and hope that in future lives, we can once again be with him.

Also, there is our good friend, Lama Ole who, year after year, has stayed with us, bringing one band of Northern Europeans after another to our home for mini-encampments. Ole is a jewel. He is also a revolutionary and rogue - no doubt attributable to his Viking heritage. I am honored to say that I have known him possibly longer than anyone in America. For over

35 years I have studied with him, practiced with him, ridden through various storms of accusations about his teaching methods and behavior. In all of this I see an example of a solid practitioner, totally committed to His Holiness Karmapa and willing to carry out His Holiness' command in as skillful a way as he can - even if that way challenges established lines of authority or policy. I remember the first time I received a blessing from the Sixteenth Karmapa. To this day, I feel that same energy with Ole. And, from the energy of the phowa that he did for Shamara twenty-seven years ago, individuals and groups in the thousands have come to him around the world to learn phowa. In 2009, when we came together at the phowa course that he was teaching in San Diego, we reflected on this – on how it all began.

A few years ago in one of my books, *The Wisdom of The Buddhist Masters: Common and Uncommon Sense*, I interviewed a number of Buddhist masters on their views of current events and what they saw happening on the planet over the next 50 to 100 years. Their comments were varied and provocative. And it was clear that we are living in a time of great turmoil; what some call a Dark Age. Yet, their words were re-assuring and, at the same time, challenging. In a world that is marked by impermanence, unless we can fully comprehend our lives and the preciousness of our human birth, we shall not have the foresight and clarity to make positive changes for ourselves or the world as we see it. In my mind, one of the features of our lives that we need to address and learn to approach more healthily and holistically, and accept is dying and death. That is why I decided to let more people know about Shamara's and our journey.

While it was the Dharma teachings that we received from Khenpo Rinpoche, Shamar Rinpoche, Lama Ole, and others great Buddhist teachers that informed and made possible our Shamara's Rebirth into Pure Land and our own transformations, from the point of sacred outlook - the highest view of Buddhism - and from the profound and direct lessons we learned from Shamara's Rebirth Into Pure Land – everyone and, everything is our teacher. Everything radiates Buddha nature. Teachers and teachings abound. All are reminders that the Pure Land is always here, always now.

To awaken to and become committed to this vision until we truly embrace the world in this way is the only goal worth striving for.

To do so or not to do so is in our hands. It is up to us.

Day of the Medicine Buddha
February 11th, 2011

PART TWO:

PREPARING FOR OUR FINAL, AMAZING JOURNEY

WHAT HAPPENS WHEN WE DIE

I have heard Tibetan masters and doctors say, "The first sign of death is birth."

Once we are conceived and the egg starts dividing and multiplying into the being that we shall be known as in the various ages and stages of our lives, we are on a one-way trajectory to an inevitable demise. The Buddhist tradition strongly emphasizes that as human sentient beings, we need to understand and accept IMPERMANENCE as a feature of life. If we do not, then we will not treasure our lives or the lives of others properly and more than likely take unnecessary risks along the way.

Although through taking the subtle pulses of a patient it is said that a Tibetan doctor can ascertain how many breaths we have until the end of our lives and Eastern astrologers can all but pinpoint the moment of death, most of us do not have nor are surrounded by people with such knowledge. At best, most of us will hopefully learn the lessons that will make us more resilient and positive in our intentions and actions over the course of our lives, AND prepare us for a graceful exit. In this I am reminded of the movie "Toy Story," where the hero, Woody, shouts out to Buzz Lightyear, "Watch out, you're going to crash." To which Buzz says, "I'm not crashing. I'm falling with style." Cascading through the process of birth, sickness - and for those who make it – old age, we all arrive at the same point where exit is the only option. But whilst this is an inevitable fact of having a body the road we take and how we travel upon that road does matter. As I have seen in my hospice work, we die as we have lived. The more conscious we are, the more we learn to "fall with style," the more that way of being and its benefits will be seen in our final moments.

In her revolutionary work, Dr. Elizabeth Kubler-Ross was able to document 5 stages in the process of us coming to terms with dying and death. These are (1) denial, (2) anger, (3) bargaining, (4) depression, and finally (5) acceptance. Especially in our technologically oriented medical system which sees death as an unwelcome guest, acknowledgement of this mental/emotional process opened some hearts and minds, thus bringing into existence what we now have as the modern hospice movement. But, I would venture to say that regardless of how in tune or out of tune any culture and medical system is with dying and death, these 5 stages present themselves in one fashion or another, in various levels of intensity. For most of us, it's so hard to let go of all to which we have become accustomed – even if it has been unpleasant. Yet, I would also contend that the degree to which the medical/healing system of a culture understands the body in both its gross and subtle aspects coming into and traveling through the various stages of actual dying makes the five stages of Kubler-Ross less or more acceptable and workable.

In the eastern medical traditions of Chinese medicine and Indian and Tibetan Ayurveda, it is said that there are Five Phases to the dying process. There is a pattern that includes physical, emotional, and spiritual dimensions. To most of us, some of these signs are imperceptible. We might even contest that they are even there. But, this has more to do with our cultural biases and the emotions of the time than the truth of the matter. Once we are able to overcome or at least step back from these biases, knowing and learning how to work with these phases on all levels makes this life transition that much easier for both the dying person and the loved ones he or she is leaving behind. Indeed, the journey we all must take, which always had its sadness , becomes open, resplendent, and full of unimagined possibilities. In other words: amazing – not only for what it offers us, but also because of the legacy and inspiration we grace everyone with in making our final time and actions as conscious and lovingly directed as we possibly can.

The concept of the four humors of the body is an old, but not readily applied model for looking at the body in the West. Not much is ever really talked about in such terms. But, the Eastern counter-part, what are called the Five Elements or Transformations are very much a part of the living and practiced traditions of Ayurveda and Chinese medicine. As I work more in the realm of Ayurveda as practiced in the Tibetan and Indian tradition, I shall use the names of the elements as described in these traditions. That said, because these elements or – as is more appropriate to their function - transformational stages use such names as Earth, Air, Water, Ether or Space, and Fire, it is assumed that these systems are in some ways archaic or primitive. In fact, each one of these names represents a certain energetic quality present in all phenomena and all phenomena go through two distinct cycles in how the energetic of these transformational stages work together. This is a fascinating subject which is at the core much of my life, work, and philosophy. I could go on for page after page just on this subject. Maybe some other time. For now, I want to look at these elements with respect to dying. Here I shall be describing the relationship of the elements according to Indian and Tibetan Ayurveda as well as the mind science that really is at the core of Buddhist spiritual practice.

In Indian and Tibetan Ayurveda, the Five Elements come together to form three energetic constituents known as *doshas* in Sanskrit. (There are Tibetan names for each of the following terms. But rather than making all of this complicated and stuffed with jargon that will only serve to confuse, I shall just stick with the Sanskrit.) Keeping just to the Sanskrit terms, Earth and Water come together to form what is called *Kapha*. Kapha is responsible for the solid form and density of our body. Water and Fire come together to form what is called *Pitta*. Tibetan Ayurveda actually make Pitta a triad of Water, Fire, and Air – but that is not a significant distinction to discuss here. Pitta is responsible for all metabolic processes; such as our digestion and glandular activity. Then there is *Vata* which is comprised of Air and Ether (or Space). Vata relates to our nervous system and is responsible for all forms of movement inside us (the pumping of blood, the movement of air) us as well as our walking from here to there, picking up a fork, etc…

The elements that comprise these doshas are in a dynamic tension that sustains life. All of the advice and health care practices of Indian and Tibetan Ayurveda, from dietary considerations, to herbs, to acupuncture, surgery, and so on are all devoted to maintaining the balance of the elements of each dosha. Throughout our lives, time, circumstances, and the choices we make along the way will contribute to how dynamic and optimally functioning each one of the doshas will function in sustaining us. And, inevitably, it is the breakdown between the elements of each dosha that leads us to our final moments in this life.

When we begin the dying process, the Kapha dosha, the relationship between the Earth and Water element begins to break down. This is first seen in emotional and physical symptoms related to the Earth element. At a physical level, we begin to lose our appetite and the movement of our physical body gets harder and harder. It is difficult to go from sitting or lying to standing. Our circulation begins to slow down and is at first noticed in the mottling of our feet. Massage that use to feel good no longer is welcome, especially of the feet. We start losing the control over our body functions and can at times feel like we are floating, other times, like we are sinking. We make more moaning noises and feel emotions of sadness and uncertainty. In Buddhist mind terms, as we lose our sense of touch and thus our physicality, the mental aggregate known as FEELING - our sense of contact with three-dimensional reality – begins to dissolve and we become more aware of the subtle forces around us.

We might begin to see beings or things that others do not.

As this Earth element breaks down, it de-stabilizes the Water element. We develop a sense of thirst that is unquenchable. Our eyes feel dry, our mouth sticky. We become incontinent and sleep patterns become reversed where we sleep through the day and remain awake all night. There is a greater feeling of being numb all over. The mental aggregate of PERCEPTION begins to break down and our mind feels hazy and we feel frustrated. This becomes evident as our thoughts and the connections between them become more fluid and less linear rational. We see connections between things never before experienced. As a result, our language becomes more metaphoric, which confuses our loved ones. We feel we are losing connection with them and them with us. At times, we feel like we are just being swept away by a current. As a result, we may feel fearful.

As Earth and Water made up the Kapha dosha, we are losing our sense of body. Our eye sense deteriorates and everything appears as a mirage.

As the Water element breaks down further, it de-stabilizes the Fire element. We lose our sense of smell and there is a fluctuation in our body heat. At times we feel hot, other times very cold. We at first notice this in our fingers and toes, which gradually moves towards our forehead, then our heart. Even our breath begins to feel cold and our mouth and nose get very dry. The mind aggregate of CONCEPTION dissolves as we can no longer hold onto reason or rationale. With the breakdown between Water and Fire, there is further loss of sensation and the inspiration to live or act. Our hearing deteriorates and we feel as if we are surrounded by smoke.

As Fire breaks down further, the element of Air is de-stabilized. Breathing becomes labored and all sense of body goes in and out; everything becomes a blur. We are losing or seeing the breakdown of the mental aggregate known as CONSCIOIUSNESS. The Air element is associated with our ability to understand and be connected to our own history. Thus, as this element dissolves, our life flashes before our eyes and we get to experience the truth of the illusion of time. As the relationship and balance between Fire and Air is deconstructed, the energy of desire fades as well as the distinction between you and me. We feel surrounded by sparks of light. That is why it is not uncommon for friends or loved ones to intuit or think of saying "Go to the light." The problem with this is sometimes this light feels comforting. Sometimes it does not.

Regardless, at some point, our natural breath stops. Even though our last breath goes out, this often happens slowly so what is noticed or seen is the last breath in. We have the experience as if being enveloped by a flame that goes out. The metabolic processes of the Pitta dosha that have been cooking to keep us alive are exhausted. We are clinically dead.

As the Air element further dissolves and the energy and oxygen in the system are working at a more subtle level, the Space or Ether element begins to also dissolve. The ether element is responsible for muscular movement. People may notice that our bodies twitch as we have what are known as tetanic contractions.

With the breakdown of the Vata dosha at the physical level, our body becomes very still and the final mental aggregate known as FORM and the connection to the form that we were comes to an end.

These phases and the breaking down of the elements occur over varying lengths of time and - like layers of an onion - some of the cycling through the phases happens more rapidly and at other levels more slowly. Sometimes we are aware of the gradual breakdown at a physical level, other times emotional, other times at a spiritual level. Regardless, in coming to our final terminal point, all of these will coalesce to present themselves in their entirety. And, I conjecture that if we are able to go back and look at the end-of-life moments of those who have died in accidents and even by their own hand, we can see a moving of natural forces that are both mysterious, but orderly – that aspects of the breakdown between the five elements was occurring in its own subtle, but dynamic way.

But, that is not the end of the story. There is still much going on inside our still, seemingly lifeless body. And there is still much that can be done, either by us, or with the help of others.

Breath or life force has been moving through the body up to this point. Thus, even though we have stopped willfully or naturally breathing, there is the breath that is left in our body that still possesses life force. It is still moving, but at a very subtle level. This subtle level has to do with the chakras or energy vortices in our body.

As we lie there very still, anyone looking at us might notice that we do not look vacant or not present. We actually look somewhat pensive, as if we are concentrating. And that is exactly what we are doing. Buddhist teachers say that for about 30 minutes we are in a state of *samadhi* – a state of meditative awareness. During that time, friends and loved ones are encouraged to be quite and mindful. If they feel too emotional, it is best that they leave the proximity of the body. In cultures that already have this custom, this is much easier to enforce.

This thirty-minute period is then broken down roughly into two fifteen minute segments.

In the first fifteen minutes, we become aware of the forehead, the region of the third eye or ajna chakra. This makes sense even from a western perspective because of the fact that the brain is still considered vital and that if the heart is miraculously restarted before a certain amount of time, there is no neurological damage to the brain and the person can possibly fully recover.

The Tibetan teachings say that at the forehead chakra, we experience a glowing like that of the moon. With this moonlight, we experience the passing of a number of negative emotions that are considered gross and subtle levels of anger. One might conjecture the ferocity with which we try to cling on to life. Our thoughts, our schemes come to naught and as we let go into space, the will to fight dies and the moonlight-like light moves towards our heart and dissolves.

We are then drawn to a reddish-orange sun-like light centered in our pelvis, the region of our two lowest chakras. With this sun-like light we experience the passing of emotions of passion and desire. Our

81

creative and procreative forces can do nothing to bring us back and as we let go of attachments, this sun-like light moves up towards and dissolves in our heart.

With the energies of anger and passion dissolved into our hearts, it is said that we have a clear light experience; an experience of our true nature; naked, unfettered by the negative emotions that cloud our realization of this truth. If through prayer and meditation we have become accustomed to the experience of this light and understand it to be none other than our true nature, we instantly attain Enlightenment. If we don't – and most of us do not – we become confused and overwhelmed. We black out and remain unconscious for several days.

At this point, our friends and loved ones would notice that the focus or concentration we seemed to be experiencing in that half hour fades and we begin to look as if we are no longer present. And this is more or less true for about three days. Tibetan masters say that after three days, our consciousness comes to. Although no longer in our physical body, because our consciousness was in that body for so long, we awaken with the mental habit, thus sense of having a body. But, it is not our diseased, old or decrepit body of our last days. It is the young and vibrant body of our heyday; our twenties or thirties. But, no one sees us and either with the help of those who know we are going through this or from our own conscious process, we suddenly or gradually awaken to the truth that we no longer are who we were. And we are on the journey in what is called the bardo or state between death and our next incarnation; our next rebirth.

Such a view of dying and death is so foreign to us. How would we prepare ourselves or others if this understanding was something we all knew, all shared, and would learn the skills to act with? The yogis, masters, and medical doctors and scientists of the East have studied, documented and worked with what I have described here for centuries. And many of the dying, death, and grief rituals that we see in these cultures that look so foreign to us are firmly rooted in a knowing that this part of the journey, the final moments in our current incarnation, prepare us for what happens next.

What is also said in these eastern traditions is that, as impermanence is a feature of life, we really do not know when death will occur. Thus, it makes sense to learn these things about life and the habit patterns of our own minds as soon as we are able. For at the time of dying, when so many physical and emotional forces are breaking down, changing, and dissolving, more than likely the thoughts and emotional patterns that have been most ingrained will be the ones that determine the tone and tenor of this part of our life's journey. We cannot, thus, cram for the test by learning these things at the last moment – at least easily. What makes this doubly difficult is that when our consciousness is finally dis-connected from our body, teachers say that it happens like a magnitude ten earthquake. We get shaken up. This is why few of us have all but glimmers of our previous existences; the lessons are learned and we go into the next life with patterns of probable action and reaction being more likely. But we use these assets and challenges in a new field of information – in a new body. Thus even if we have memories of our past lives, they soon fade in the immediacy of what we have to face here and now.

Understanding this and training our minds as best we can in this life gives us the greatest chance to have the habitual inclination to utilize the time and energy of our dying and transition more skillfully. At the same time, eastern teachers say that without this knowledge and practice, it is still possible to positively influence the course of a person's next destination. That is why prayers for the dying are done. That is why there is phowa.

Phowa (pronounced poh-whah) is one of the six yogas of Naropa, an Indian yogi who was one of the great masters in the Kagyu lineage of Tibetan Buddhism. It has been taught over the centuries to spiritual practitioners who want to overcome the fear of dying, become fearless in life, and have the ability to – at the time of death – spontaneously move their life force up and out of the body through the crown chakra, thus ensuring the most favorable of rebirths. In the Tibetan Buddhist world this means being born in a Buddha realm. In the Kagyu tradition of which I am a student, the goal is to go to the Pure Land known as Dewachen – the Land of Bliss – the domain of the Amitabha Buddha. The purpose of being reborn into the Amitabha's Pure Land is to reside in a place where one can – without hindrance or distraction – complete the spiritual practice of awakening, thus become a helpful being to everyone. But, as a non-Buddhist, you may have a different goal in mind. Having learned the mind-technology of the phowa practice, you could have your consciousness or the consciousness of a loved one directed to the realm or heaven of your beliefs.

In Buddhist terms, phowa engages the body and mind through the focusing of intention, joyfully opening up to a connection with a lineage of masters and practitioners who have done this practice over the centuries, following the physical and mental processes in the actual meditation as prescribed leading to the consciousness leaving the body through the highest possible energy vortex (optimally the crown chakra at the central fontanel site), and finally sharing all good feelings that arise for the welfare of everyone without exception. Once an adept has learned to do this in his or her own life, they can also develop the ability to focus on someone else at the moment of their dying, within the first 30 minutes after they died, or three days later when the deceased's consciousness wakes from the initial blackout from the death event, and propel their consciousness into that Pure Land state. Great masters can even do this for another up to 49 days after their death.

When reading this description, one might get the impression that phowa is an intervention; that it is somehow a method for avoiding heaven, hell, or whatever happens next for us – a free pass to something better if we didn't think that something better is what we had in store for ourselves. But, that is not the case.

Yogis and doctors of the East teach that between our death and our next life, there is a maximum of 49 days. Where we end up is solely based on our previous efforts. There is no promise of heaven or notion that reincarnation is a progressively positive progression and that where we end up will be better or more improved than what we have just departed from. That is up to us. However, with phowa, your consciousness leaves the physical body in the most auspicious way. In the lineage that I practice, the consciousness is projected into a state and place where whatever karmic foibles you have, you can work them out without causing anyone else any harm. Especially if you have very strong negative habits, you are protected from yourself so that all of your worst inclinations do not disturb anyone else and you can, thus, exhaust them yourself. Dewachen, The Land of Bliss, according to Buddhist tradition, is the closest and most opportune situation for us as human sentient beings to be reborn into. It is where it is most easy for us to awaken to our full potentials, realize the unlimited capacities of our minds, and experience a bliss that makes all of our future acts as newly awakened beings spontaneous and joyful. Thus, in the right time and circumstance, anyone who masters the yoga of phowa and or who has the good fortune of having their consciousness transferred by a phowa master can be reborn into Dewachen. One does not have to be a practicing Buddhist to go to Dewachen. And, judgment on who is good or bad does not matter here. Dewachen is an enlightenment training facility and each one who has the auspicious circumstance to arrive here will eventually graduate as an Awakened Being.

I want to re-iterate that using the focus and energy of the yoga of phowa doe not demand a faith in the Amitabha Buddha or Dewachen. There are many people

I know who have trained in the yoga of phowa or have requested that the phowa practice be done on their behalf who are not Buddhists. In his groundbreaking book, *The Tibetan Book of Living and Dying*, the Venerable Sogyal Rinpoche makes it quite clear that one can use the phowa exercise he offers to focus on ones relationship with God, Jesus, or the heavenly beings or realms that one has been taught in ones tradition. And, in the second chapter of Part Two, the end of the dying exercise will guide you into a phowa visualization similar to the one offered by Sogyal Rinoche which, if practiced periodically to familiarize yourself with its energetic, will be helpful for you in your ending time as well as anyone else who you may similarly attend. And while it is not the same as the actual phowa practice as described in the story of Shamara, it is effective and will even help you in your understanding of the actual phowa practice if you so chose to learn it. For that you need to be taught and authorized by a recognized phowa master. It is especially helpful to have this vigorous training if you want to include the practice of phowa as part of your dying or to help another with the same. The Useful Addresses at the end of the book provide you with information you need to contact an organization or teacher that does offer phowa training.

The Benefits of Phowa

The story of Shamara is a testimony to the beauty and power of phowa. But, I would like to emphasize what benefits you and your loved ones can gain from learning this practice.

As described in the story of Shamara, learning phowa is an initiatory process; learned from a phowa master. Anyone of any creed can learn, practice, and utilize phowa in one's own death or the death of a loved one.

Learned properly, when periodically practicing the yogic methods of phowa in preparation for when dying arrives upon you, you will notice that you feel clearer, lighter in your being. Fear of your own dying is eroded and confidence grows.

Perhaps your time of dying will come at the end of a long life or after a chronic disease. But it can also come suddenly; a massive heart attack, brain aneurism, or an accident. Thus you may be at home with loved ones. But, you may also be in a hospital, walking down the street, at work, in a car or airplane. Regardless of the circumstance, phowa will help because as you periodically practice its yogic methods, you are creating a subtle and powerful habit in your being that will allow your mind or consciousness energy to naturally leave your body through the crown chakra and go to the most auspicious place you can imagine. For Buddhists, this will be the Pure Land – a Buddha realm. But this next place for you might be heaven, paradise, or realms of light. Furthermore if you become an adept of this practice, you will also be able to direct the energy of a friend or loved one in the same manner, even remotely. When I was working for hospice and after a few of the nurses from the hospice I worked for also learned phowa, we would call each other and do phowa from other locales for our respective clients. The red spot or broken blood vessels on the crown of the head – one of the signs for phowa –

happened within the half hour after death for many of these clients.

In the seeming hopelessness so many feel in the moment of death, it may seem just a comfort to think that phowa makes a difference. But, in seeing the signs, witnessing the miracles, and hearing stories of others, I know that phowa works. It makes a beneficial difference and I have every confidence in encouraging everyone I know to avail yourselves of such training if it becomes available to you.

Regardless of whether you do learn phowa visualization as described by Sogyal Rinpoche or the yoga of phowa as was done for Shamara, what I offer here as background information, wisdom from the many teachers I have had the great privilege of learning from over the years, will be indispensable to you as you prepare for and inevitably face your final moments. What follows next is a preparation-for-dying exercise that serves to bring to life and make visceral the various body, emotional, and spiritual dimensions of the dying experience as I have just described them.

AN EXERCISE TO PREPARE YOU OR A LOVED ONE FOR THE FINAL JOURNEY

The exercise you are about to participate in was inspired by the work of Stephen Levine. After his book, *A Year to Live*, was published, many hospices nationwide began to run "One Year to Live" programs where participants would elect to live for the following year as if it was their last. Periodically, participants would meet in groups to discuss what they were going through, running into, letting go of, in this thought provoking process. I encourage anyone to contact their local hospice organization to see if one of these groups is available. It is well worth your time.

A friend of mine had elected to do this exercise. Periodically she would mention to me what she was going through as a result. I was curious about the process, but wondered how she expected to end the year. So, I bluntly asked her, "What is your drop dead date?"

She did not know what to say. As far as she knew, people just sort of finished the process and gradually returned to their everyday lives, albeit changed in a very uplifting way.

I wasn't satisfied with this and in some ways, her comments lead me to believe that neither was she. So, I constructed a "dying day" scenario for her, based on the Five Elements and the process of phowa.

I have now led professional, religious, and lay groups in a number of settings through this exercise in my dying and death workshops. It is structured to include guided visualizations and contemplations intended to help you look at your body and emotions more fully and help you become more appreciative of some of the dynamics we go through as we transition out of our current incarnation and move onto what will be our next.

Although Phases Two and Three are designed for you to be able to use them as part of your own or someone else's real dying process, Phase One is more of a contemplation that is mostly for your consideration here and now. It will also inform you of what we all cycle through in the dissolving of our own elements. Thus, whereas Phase Two and Three can be read aloud in our final moments, Phase One, is a contemplation, something you can reflect upon and observe. Simply put, the time frame of the dissolution of the elements can vary considerably and occurs almost as if in layers. Thus knowing when to read it would be very hard to determine and, in the flow of what we go through as we are actively in the dying process, such a script may just be irritating.

Thus, to do this exercise in the general course of your life, there are any number of ways you can elect to do it. If you want to do it by yourself, as a form of contemplation, set a couple of hours aside or go through it incrementally over a period of days to fully absorb and digest the considerations that each portion of the exercise directs you to contemplate.

Another approach is to do this exercise either by yourself or with a group of loved ones, friends, or colleagues with an appointed reader, a caregiver. For those of you who wish, a CD of this process is available.

PREPARATION:

If you plan on doing the entire exercise, select a time of day where you have two to three hours to fully immerse yourself in the process. And, it is best to have some quiet time, either by yourself or with those you have shared the exercise with afterwards.

Dress in loose and comfortable clothing. Remove your watch if you have one. And prepare a comfortable place where you will, during the body of the exercise, sit or retire to. This is where you are going to die.

THE EXERCISE
PHASE ONE:
I. FINAL CELEBRATION MEAL

I have observed that just prior to become imminent, many a dying person suddenly appears to develop an appetite. They want to eat and may loved ones are led to believe that this means that their loved one is recovering.

In fact, it takes a lot of energy to die. And it is almost as if the dying person is packing in the calories to prepare for what lies ahead.

So, to begin the exercise, make yourself a great snack, breakfast, or lunch or whatever. Do not be at all conceptual about what is good or not good for you, what has calories, etc…Name the foods you would like for the celebration – no holds barred in terms of price or combination, no matter how seemingly ridiculous. Enjoy (But remember: For the exercise, don't make yourself so stuffed and uncomfortable that you can't lie down for the next 60 plus minutes!)

II.   PROCLAMATION: (10 minutes to do this segment of the exercise)

Each of us has a legacy; what we have done, what we not done, what we have accomplished, what we wished we had accomplished, and so on. In general, as part of our final days, it is healthy to take time for a life review, a getting clear on what your life has meant and what you have and want to leave behind.

That said, in the context of this exercise and following your feast, dedicate your death. Contemplate what you would like your epitaph to be. Imagine that this is your last and final conscious attempt to define the meaning of the life you are leaving, what it has meant to you, and in what ways you want to see your death be of value. (examples: Think of an emotion that has been really hard to let go of and make a prayer that with you this particular emotional affliction dies for all beings. Or, it may be a physical problem. What would you like to see more of on the planet? What would you like to see less of? Dedicate the energy of your dying in seeing the world that way.)

At the end of your PROCLAMATION, you speak no more. These are your final words.

(If you are in a group or have a Caregiver attending to you, you are completely under their direction. There is NO negotiation on time. IT IS TIME. You should now go to wherever you will sit or lie as you go through the dying process. (If you need to use the bathroom, this is the time to do it.) What we are simulating here is the fact that at some point in our dying process, we shall be unable to move or speak. Here, we are consciously making that decision so that we can tune in to the deeper levels of contemplation that will be asked of you here.

III. WORKING WITH THE ELEMENTS: (30 minutes)
During this portion, the Caregiver will address you by your first name as they go through the dissolution of the elements. (Modify if you are in a group – just make general commands.)What follows is a guided visualization and all you need to do is read or follow along...

"You are now resting where you need to be____. At this time you become aware of the very surface of your body. Feel the skin over every surface. This puts you in touch with your EARTH element. As you breathe in and out, soften your attention to your body and allow this sense of contact with the surface of your body to become hazier. Allow yourself to sink deeper and deeper onto the surface that you are resting on. NOTICE that all your concepts about the world, about yourself become less solid. You do not hold on to any concrete idea. Thoughts just come and go. There is no more judgment about what you think or what you hear.

As the EARTH element dissolves for you, you may notice twinges of doubt, of uncertainty about what you have done, what you are doing, what it all means or does not mean – and this puts you in touch with levels of previously undiscovered layers of sadness as you let go.

But, as you let go more and more, feel a new openness and unimpeded connection with what is around you. Feel a natural empathy in the presence of inseparability not bound by your previous views of your human limitations."

(Allow 2 minutes to pass, then…)

"Letting go of the solidity of your body, become aware of the moistness inside and around you. Notice how you may be thirsty or not. You also become aware of a sense of numbness to your body as you can no longer fixate on its solidity. As you are now more in touch with the WATER element, notice how your mind floats - how connections between ideas and concepts flow together, then apart. Nothing is fixed as you find yourself encountering deeper levels of your consciousness.

Touching the WATER element puts you in touch with your hesitation, your over cautiousness, the root of which is fear of non-being, of the truth of your insubstantiality. And, as you let go into this, a deeper knowing of your inseparability from the flow of life around you becomes more obvious."

(To Caregiver: Allow 2 minutes to pass, then notice if your partner or the participants look cold or hot. Either way have a blanket available. Pay attention to whether you think he/she is hot or cold.)

"As you go deeper into yourself and as you are dissolving your connection to what is at all solid puts you in touch with feelings of warmth and coldness, both within you and around you. Notice these feelings starting at your feet and move slowly up your body. You are encountering your FIRE Element. There is now no more sense of separation between you and what is around you. There is not even a concept about that. It just is. It is real and it is insubstantial and your mind dances between images of being and non-being, of shadow and light. You are more aware of the light around you, but also the light within.

In FIRE, you get in touch with your listlessness, the flitting nature of your mind and impressions of having a body. As you attempt to let go at this level, you encounter anxiety, even panic – yet you breathe in and breathe out and go on. And, as you go on, the light becomes stronger and your passion for holding on to what is small and personal gives way to a warmth that spreads out, a compassion that begins to dawn based on wisdom – of knowing what is and what is not. And your heart grows and becomes fuller and fuller. You rest in a joy that would normally make you dance and sing. But here, you cannot dissipate or move that joy but through your being. You are that joy."

(Allow another 2 minutes, then…)

"You are now only aware of your breath. It comes in and goes out. All is subtle, all is just breath. You are now in touch with the AIR Element and only conscious of consciousness itself.

And silently, as you breathe in and breathe out, review your life. Allow impressions to rise up naturally. Notice where you have had your greatest attachments – what you have held onto in this life. Notice what lingers on - what you want to hold onto; people, places, things, ideas about yourself. See how it is your attachment and not the objects of your attachment that has limited you, brought desperation, made you act in a distracted manner. Breathe in and breathe out and allow your mind to expand. All of what and whom you are attached to are not your mind – who you are. They are just impressions that come and go. What must you learn from them? With each breath out just let go of holding on.

Notice now what in your past has brought up for you frustration, irritation, even, and anger. Examine your past, as far back as your mind will allow. What has created the most heat in you, burned up your positive energy, made you feel weak at times? Look at where you have exploded at someone, carried a grudge, caused harm with even the slightest intent to do so. Acknowledge this in yourself and let go. Release all your fixation to these moments in your life. Feel the heat of pettiness diminish as you breathe and out.

Notice now at the edges of your mind what has not been given proper attention. Look over your life and look at what you have ignored, put on the back burner, seen as unimportant or not worth your time or attention, what you have turned a blind eye to. Where have you let yourself or others down? See these events, these images in your mind and let go. Allow remorse to dissolve into a commitment to never look the other way in times to come…

What drags on your mind; stiff ideas, illusions, stories you tell yourself about this person, that place, this group, even the stories you have about yourself? See them as a play arising from the past. Remain only committed to seeing yourself carry into your new life the lessons of your history."

(Allow another 2 minutes to pass, then…)

"Freed of the residues of your past, freed of holding on any more, you expand into the SPACE around you. You feel the space within you. You have no will to move. You just lie there and – as best you can – you remain present to this moment, nothing more." You breathe free, breathe relaxed. There is nothing more to do. You just lie in the vastness of possibility.

The active physical dying process has now come to its final point. You have now passed on into the next stage that awaits you. Allow yourself to be in the quiet, just with your breath as you are directed to look at deeper and more subtle levels of your existence.

PHASE TWO: DISSOLVING OF THE LIGHTS WITHIN:
[NOTE: As mentioned earlier, this script could be read to the deceased right after the moment of death. It would be read over the course of approximately 36 minutes, divided into 2 fifteen minute, then 1 six-minute segment. At the same time, if we or the person attending us knew phowa, we would not read or do

this Phase Two portion, but go directly to working with the phowa. But, if you feel uncomfortable with or do not remember or have the time to do or work with the phowa, reading or recalling this script is immensely useful to the transitioning person.]

(Caregiver: In actual dying the following script would be read to the now deceased person, unless doing phowa. For the exercise, allow 3-5 minutes for each of the first two segments, then 2 minutes for the last segment.)

Script for the Time after the Moment of Physical Dying
(segment 1) "Beloved_____, at this time you must clearly understand that your outer breath has stopped and that you will not return to the life that you have just departed. It is time to move on and even though we love you dearly and are saddened by your departure, we want to be of help to you in this important time.

Right now, you are deep within your being. Your worldly breath is gone, but the true energy of who you are remains for now within your still form. Your look is deep and thoughtful and we know that you can hear us, whether we speak these words out loud or within our minds. So please, pay attention.

For some time, you will witness from within a moon-like light that is traveling from the top of your head and is making its way to your heart through the central spiritual channel of your body. This moon-like light is a white essence that has always been a part of you. It is your male energy. As this energy moves towards your heart, 33 different feelings associated with any anger you have ever felt dissolve. Beloved_____, this is time for you to let go of any aggressiveness you have ever felt in defending your life. Just let it go and rest in the joyfulness and light that you are beginning to feel."

(Read at least twice. Then, in this exercise, allow 2 minutes of silence…)

(segment 2) "After this moon-like light has dissolved into your heart, Beloved, a radiant orange sun-like light begins to travel from just below your navel and makes its way towards your heart through the central spiritual channel of your body. This sun-like radiance is a red essence that has always been a part of you. It is your female energy. As this energy moves towards your heart, 40 disturbing feelings associated with any clinging you have ever felt dissolve. Beloved_____, this is time for you to let go of any attachments you have ever felt in holding onto your life and to others in your life. Just let go and open up to the limitless nature of your mind freed of all boundaries."

(Repeat once more, then allow 2 minutes…)

(segment three) "Finally, Beloved_____, as these white and red essences meet in your heart, the imminence of your enlightened nature will be at hand. 7 forms of cloudiness, of ignorance about who you are and the nature of all that has ever been around you, dissolves. It will be pure darkness, Beloved, but soon will dawn as the realm of Clear Light. This is your true nature, Beloved_____. Do not shy away from this experience. Do not get confused. Allow yourself to joyfully open to the limitless nature that is you. This is your time. This is so special. Allow yourself to be at one with the Clear Light that is none other than who you have always been and now get to experience without any restrictions. Rest in this vibrant truth, Beloved, and know that we love you and wish nothing less than this for you."

(Caregiver: Remain silent for 3-5 minutes)

PHASE III:
PHOWA EXERCISE:
    [NOTE: As mentioned above, if in our real dying situation we have been trained in phowa or have someone attending us who knows phowa, the practice of or reading of the phowa for the deceased would happen immediately when the physical breath has stopped. We would not wait to do the visualization as presented in Phase Two. But, here, in our simulation exercise, one can follow one with the other. Because in truth, if one did not have the opportunity to do phowa at the time of actual dying, the yoga of phowa practice would be done for us three days, then during or up to forty-nine days after our transition anyway.
    What follows is a modified version of the phowa exercise found in Sogyal Rinpoche's *The Tibetan Book of Living and Dying*. I am indebted to his inspiration and the support along the way from his Spiritual Dying Network. Please bear in mind that as a phowa exercise, it is not the same as the actual phowa practice that was done for Shamara or that can be learned from a qualified phowa master.]

(Contemplate on or have the Caregiver read the following script of Phowa to you...)

Part ONE

"You who have been in the life you have left behind known as _____, as you lie still, please listen to what I am to say. Please try to follow along and place your heart and intention into what I am about to ask you to do…

In the sky in front of you, visualize and call upon the embodiment of whatever truth and love you have faith in. Perhaps it is God or a being who you see most as the embodiment of God for you. Maybe it is a Buddha, or a prophet, but definitely someone or something you have the greatest confidence in to help you in this time. See them in a form that radiates or appears as radiant light. Feel their presence entirely, around and within you. They embody or represent truth, wisdom, compassion, love… Do not be concerned if you do not see them clearly – just fill your heart with their presence and trust that they are here for you."

Part TWO

"Now, please hear me one who was been known as _____… Please focus your mind, your heart, your very essence on the presence of this radiant being and pray from deep with you…

'*Through your blessing, power, grace, and guidance, through the power of the light that streams through you;*

May all my negative actions and behaviors, destructive emotions, confusion, and resistances and blockages to knowing my full potential even in this late hour be purified and removed;

May I know myself forgiven for all the harm I may have thought or done in this life and the residues of such from all my lives since beginningless time;

Through my intention and action here, may I realize the benefits of this profound phowa practice, and die a good and peaceful death,

And through the triumph of skillfully mastering and embracing my own death, may my efforts bring benefit and blessings to all other beings, living or dead.'

Now imagine that the radiant divine presence before you that you have called upon is so moved by your heartfelt prayer that they respond with a loving smile and send out love and compassion in streams of light from their heart. As these beams touch and enter you, they cleanse and purify all your negative actions and behavior, conflicted emotions, and confusion and resistance which are the causes of suffering. Feel and imagine that this light surrounds you and is in every cell of your body. Notice anywhere in your body or mind there is darkness, places where the light does - not get to initially. Breathe and relax, allow the light to move into these places as well. Allow yourself to feel totally immersed in this radiance.

In this radiant state, know that you are now completely purified and healed by the light streaming from the divine presence. Imagine that the illusion of any distinction or separation between the light and your own body, itself created by your own previous actions, now completely dissolves. You are a body of light.

And, this body of light now soars into the sky and directly merges and become inseparable from the radiant presence of light that you have called upon.

Rest in this awareness of oneness with this presence for as long as possible."

(Allow for 5 minutes of relaxation and quiet.)

(Caregiver [or if you have done this exercise on your own]: encourage the person/s practicing to slowly move his/her body and prepare for coming back into everyday life. The following script can serve towards that end...)

"Once again, bring your awareness to your slow and gentle breathing and imagine that you have been on a long journey through time and space. Continue to breathe in a relaxed way and become more conscious of the surface of your body and the contact it has with the ground you are sitting or resting upon. As you come more fully into your body, allow the lessons and experiences of the past hour or more sink in. You have practiced going on your final, amazing journey and you awaken with a new or revived awareness that stirs and deepens within you. It is like coming into a new body and mind state – a rebirth.

Reflect on this for a few moments as you stretch and move yourself in preparation to move into your ordinary activity."

Such a practice is physically, emotionally, and spiritually moving. Drink a full glass of cool water and do not rush into any activity directly afterwards that is too stressful or intense.

You might want to journal your experiences. If you did this with a Caregiver and/or group of friends, think of having some processing get-togethers to share experiences, support each other.

And, I would be happy to hear from any one or group about their experiences in doing this process.

PART THREE:

BEING IN THE
TIME OF DYING
PRACTICAL GUIDANCE IN
DYING AND DEATH

THE YOU WHO YOU HAVE
ALWAYS BEEN

In teaching his students, Korean Zen Master Seung Sahn use to tell them to focus on their breath. As they breathed in, they were instructed to pose themselves the question, "Who am I?" And, as they breathed out, they were suppose to offer themselves a truly Zen response; "Don't know." Many – if not all of Master Seung Sahn's teachings were about "don't know mind."

Of course, we are taught from an early on in one manner or another – by parents, teachers, priests, rabbis, gurus, friends, but especially from our own inner voice – that we need to learn about and know who we are. "Know thyself;" such a simple call to action that is really a life-long lesson. For, every time we think we know who we are, something new or different or challenging comes along to rattle our confidence, our certainty.

This is especially true if you are someone who takes seriously the intent of such a quest. Thus, so much of contemplative and meditative practice has at its core this life-long conundrum. Nevertheless, if this dilemma has not seemingly or obviously surfaced to intrude on your life, it certainly makes itself known in the process of our dying.

This happens for each of us in our dying, regardless of whether you die when you are young or old, die quickly or over a long drawn out process, whether you are in pain or at peace, or if death is what you expect or it creeps up on you when you are not looking. Probably because of the fact that it is inevitable, the wisdom traditions of the world try to condition us to the fact that regardless of how it comes, it is – for certain – expected. Not knowing how or when or why makes some knowledge of the dying process indispensible.

In all of his meditations, phowa master Lama Ole always draws meditations to a close by reminding us that we are <u>not</u> our bodies, but rather, that we <u>have</u> our bodies. Our bodies can be a source of power, delight, and action when well prepared and focused. But in the end, they <u>will</u> fail us. Thus to solely identify ourselves as being our power, our delight our prowess, or any of our capabilities will inevitably lead us to disappointment as our bodies fall away from the irreducible "who I am" that you are.

Preparing one's mind for this inevitability is so vital. Yet prepared or not, the letting go of expectations of what we use to be able to do but no longer can is very hard. The Danes, says Lama Ole, have a saying that our last shirt has no pockets. When we die, we are stripped down to our most basic. There are no more tricks or gimics, no pockets or sleeves for something magical to ward off what we must face. No longer a doer, we are reduced down to being. Dying is our ultimate test in knowing who we are – who we have always been.

Unless you have been tested by a personal tragedy at a young age, the gravity of such notions as I have just lain out may seem exaggerated. But, having worked with both an aging and dying population, the impact of losing energy, strength, hearing or sight, sexual expressiveness, control of one's bladder or bowels demands a letting go that few who have not gone through such can fully or are willing to empathize with. Letting go of expectation - of what one may have defined as a part of who you are, those very capacities that have been heretofore assumed to be there for you and have contributed to helping you to define yourself in relation to others, work, productivity, your very contribution to society – takes a tenacity of spirit to both accept and endure as now being true from this point forth and which will, no doubt progress. And the decline and loss of such challenges our definitions of dignity and self worth.

In this regard, *life reviews* are a valuable exercise; sitting down for yourself or with an elder or dying person so that one can chronicle or have chronicled for them their lives. This works for many, fleshing out history, the wherefores and whys, providing perspective and new insights. It can also enrich future generations. It provides legacy. And for some traditions this is as far as working with aging and dying goes in terms of meaning – the meaning of our lives.

But, such legacies are about function and performance. They are an identification with our bodies rather than having our bodies. Thus, at this stage, with the legacy passed on – which no doubt can provide relief and be of enormous value to oneself and others – what now? Do we wait it out in an in-between state, no longer alive the way we were, but not dead yet? What now? Is there meaning in our immanence and how we face it, the loss of all functions, the rasping of our breath, and the silence and stillness that come when we breathe no more? Are these just physiological events? Or, are they, too, part of the legacy of our lives, something to note, but also something that contributes to the wholeness of our lives? Standing witness in these moments, my answer to this is, yes.

Backing up, though, and just looking at the letting go in the aging process and what precedes immanence in the active dying process, where memory and expression are possible, sharing ones legacy can soften the passing of our capacities and abilities. But, if Kubler-Ross' stages are to be adhered to [(1) denial, (2) anger, (3) bargaining, (4) depression, and finally (5) acceptance] in our stumbling towards acceptance, there also needs to be lamentation. There needs to be mourning. Such mourning is a very human part and expression of acceptance.

Grieving is what we as humans do as we let go of a loved one and are left holding within ourselves their legacy. And, just as much as this applies to individuals, it is equally true to the once trusted and beloved functions and abilities within us. To come even closer to who we are rather than holding on to what we were, we must – in our own way – allow a healthy expression of grief and lamentation to wash us clean of our expectations and deliver us into a more naked state of our irreducible being. We drop our functions and facades along the way and become the person underneath it all.

In this process, probably the fiercest journey we have ever taken in the process of self discovery and awakening, dying leads us to the experience our finest hour. Such an hour may not make the history books. We may not like them and they may not be what others want to remember about us. But, in our dying, we employ whatever physical abilities we have, along with every mental and spiritual device we have cultivated in our lives. And in this time we learn how well they have served us and whether they will help us to pass through the door of what will happen next and our ability to embrace whatever it is that we encounter. And that is something only we can know. If we as those attending to the dying stand witness to and can support our loved ones through this transition, we shall have learned so much more about who our loved one was. We shall also know so much more about ourselves.

The milestones of our life, certainly birth, but also other significant markers of our lives, are awe evoking events. They may, in the chronicles of who we have been even amazing. But nothing brings it all together like our passing If ever there was an amazing moment to our lives, this is it. And all the more so if we created within ourselves the capacities to be as conscious as we can be when the time comes.

Shamara's story and everything I have offered up to this point has been to provide intellectual, emotional, and spiritual information, inspiration, and support for you in being conscious to and participating in your passing. But, this book and what it offers you would fall short if it did not offer some advice or suggestions from the holistic traditions I have studied on the physical dimension of this event. For, *we die in the flesh.* We are embodied and the cascading and collapse of our various bodily organs and systems can so easily grab our full attention. Consider how focused we get when a hammer lands on our thumb, or when a raging fever makes our minds whizz around in tight spirals of obsessive thought. Then imagine what it is like within us when every single system is failing, churning, gasping. Certainly, our mental and spiritual preparedness will make these events have a greater or lesser impact on how conscious and at peace we remain with the process. That has been the main point of so much of what has been presented thus far. But, we need to take embodiment seriously. It is prudent to have the wisdom and the means to support the body as best one can.

Of course, there are so many ways in which we can die. There is no possible way to address every possible contingency. Thus, the practical suggestions presented must be modified and used in accordance with and support the circumstance in which the dying takes place. Some of this information the one dying can use and prepare with. But, for the most part, I shall be addressing those who will be present at and stand witness to our passing.

BEING PRESENT, BEING USEFUL, AND STANDING WITNESS

I believe that there is something karmic about who is or not with each and every one of us when we die. By this I mean some kind of connection that allows us to be in the presence of or participate in some way in another's transition. One might think that this has to do with family or loved ones and sometimes this is true. But, I have seen wives and others dear to the dying who have been in attendance for days on end go out to take a drink of water, only to return to find that their loved one has slipped away. I have watched people come out of comas when a friend or significant person from their past flies in from another part of the country and walks through their door. In a similar way, I have seen them die when that person has left, as if whatever needed to transpire had occurred and was complete.

In all of this I view the event of dying as a portal between two states of being. It is an energetic that the dying person stands in the middle of as the guest of honor. They become like the center of a great vortex or mandala which has its own divine time and rhythm in which people dance in and go out in accordance with the whatever part they need to play in the final expressions of the dying person's life. In this moment I do not believe that nature, God, or whatever divine forces that so eloquently display themselves in the

115

symmetry and symphony of life leave anything to chance. This is why I titled one of my books on dying *Perfect Endings*. For, I contend, each ending is perfect for each and every individual – no matter how it appears from the outside.

Up until this point, I have focused mostly on the emotional and spiritual dimensions of our dying. But, for anyone who is in attendance to a loved one – or anyone for that matter – there is so much that needs to be done to help a person die in as pain free and peaceful a manner as is possible. In this section, I focus on physically attending to a person.

As this can be an emotionally difficult thing to do for some, it may just be that to be a mother, a wife, husband, son, or friend and be able to relate to your loved one in that manner, that attending to the various physical needs they have – bathing, cleaning bedpans or helping with a catheter, administering medication is something you want to leave to professionals, to a hospice staff or those trained to do such who you have confidence in. Do not judge yourself harshly if this is the case for you. Indeed, having the presence of hospice can be a tremendous relief and give you the emotional reserves to be with your loved one in the way that the both of you would want or prefer.

Thus, when it comes to the medical aspect of dying in the west, I encourage people to use hospice nurses and other levels of their assistance. Beyond the vital physical tasks and levels of support that hospice professionals are masters at, there are many lifestyle and comfort measures you can learn to offer that will support the peace and sacredness of this time for the dying one and yourself. These methods I would like to share with you in this chapter.

I want to emphasize here that what I am suggesting in the advice that follows is in keeping with the many holistic traditions I have studied and have practiced in general and in particular, in the time of dying and death. Most can compliment the many palliative care approaches that hospice can offer. But, I encourage each and every one of you to utilize whatever methods you have most confidence in. And, when in doubt, consult with your physician or the hospice team.

PAIN and AGITATION

Over the years, whenever the discussion of death has come up in conversation, people will often comment that they are not afraid of dying. What they <u>are</u> afraid of is the pain and suffering in the dying process itself. Thus, the first topic I would like to address is pain. As I have done this more extensively in my book, *Perfect Endings*, here I just want to focus on what you can do for yourself or another with respect to pain.

Pain is a very subjective thing. Depending on one's strength, stage in the dying process, and state of mind, the same markers of pain can be viewed as mild or horrible . So much of this subjectivity will be monitored most from within with respect to emotional and spiritual preparedness and the necessary mental flexibility on the midst of it all. And, one of the main suggestions I have for this presentation has to do with this aspect. But, for now, I want to focus on the basics lifestyle dimensions around death and dying that can be attended to alleviate or mollify pain and ease agitation.

HYDRATION

Throughout the dying process, food and hydration will become issues that need to be addressed and constantly modified. Thus, I shall start here – beginning with hydration.

In the exercise I presented earlier, I mentioned the dissolution of the water element and some of its physical and emotional components. One aspect just touched upon in that exercise was the appearance of what is clinically called Sundowners Syndrome. In this situation, the autonomic nervous system, governed by the water element, begins to malfunction. In a time of rest at night, the person cannot sleep. They become more alert. Then during the day, the reverse occurs. Often, sleep medication and other sedative-type drugs. Some that are recommended are of little avail. And, then there are the ones that will knock the person out, which is possibly more helpful to the care giver than the dying person, themselves. Regardless of the success or lack of success of medication in this time, one aspect of discomfort for the dying person remains with this reversal in the water element; an increasing thirst.

Old age and the onset of clear decline as evidenced in the dying process comes with increased dryness, hence thirst. Add to this the fact that so many mood altering and painkilling drugs have a tendency to be drying to the body, especially the colon. As the colon becomes drier, waste matter gets more stuck, leading to bloating, gas, and constipation and their related discomfort. In oriental medicine this dryness has other effects beyond the colon and its discomfort. The dryness and gas build up begin to impact the muscles and joints, thus creating pains that move all around the body, pausing agitation. Thus the issue of thirst and proper hydration become a critical component of gentle palliative care.

In the tradition of Ayurveda, there are two ways to approach this. One is through quality hydration, the other through lubrication. In this, consider this car analogy: Think of what keeps a car engine from burning up; a full radiator and a good supply of the right kind of oil as a lubricant between critical parts.

Regarding hydration, avoid drinks with a lot of sugar or corn syrup. They'll make the dying person more thirsty. Gatorade or some better natural electrolyte equivalent would be a better choice on many levels. It is also wise to keep drinks either room temperature, warm, or hot. Iced drinks are best avoided. However, after chemotherapy and radiation for cancer treatment, there is an almost insatiable desire for ice. But even in this situation, try to be moderate. Offer cool water instead.

When it comes to lubrication and oils in the immediacy of dying, now is not the time to worry about cholesterol. In fact, the whole trend in elder care to decrease oil and fat consumption in the diet is misguided and generally wrong.

Especially with the constipation and bloating that comes with so many pain and mood medications, it is wise to keep a quality oil in the diet; sesame, sunflower, and olive oils in and on foods, and perhaps omega 3 rich fish oil if the person does not mind the taste. Beyond diet, however, quality vegetable oils such as sunflower, olive, and sesame can also be rubbed on the body. Ayurveda encourages the elderly to give themselves an oil massage every day. And, in the ancient tradition of hospice care in Europe, patients would be anointed with oil. This was more than just a sacrament. Our skin ingests oil. This oil is digested by the body and helps in the overall lubrication of the body within and without. Further comment on massage will be made shortly.

Good hydration and quality lubrication can go a long way in relieving all of the symptoms I have mentioned above. And, like all such recommendations when it comes to the dying process, the parameters of what these mean will change and change again as a person approaches immanency. More importantly, they should be offered in a manner that is acceptable to the patient themselves. For as the person nears death, they will be less capable of swallowing. Thus the hydration recommendations become moot. In such a time, nurses recommend helpers to provide small sips, which may come down to the swab of a moistened q-tip. In the case of my own father, I was able to relieve his parched mouth and throat by drawing up small amounts of water into a needleless hypodermic syringe, placing its tip between his lips, and squirting it very rapidly so that it was delivered like a spray. This could also be done with a bottle that has an atomizing pump.

NUTRITION

Another issue in working with pain and providing comfort is nutrition.

One of the first signs of decline heading towards immanence as explained in the exercises is the breakdown of the Earth element. Associated with this element is eating, our appetite, and sense of taste.

As this element becomes weaker and weaker, we want to eat less. We may still have a concept in our minds of how much we want and what we think would taste good. But then we take a few bites of what someone brings us only discover that we really can't eat it all. And sometimes, our taste buds have become so changed that what we thought we really wanted just doesn't taste right.

For most of us our eating has a strong social dimension. Consequently, these changes and turning away from the stew your wife lovingly made, the cake your best friend has always shared with you and known as your favorite, the type of food and drink your friends or beloved have shared with and offered you for years are no longer savored and celebrated. This brings distress on all sides. And as a symbol of one's bond with others drops away, it is replaced by sense loss and sadness.

Thus to serve the needs of your loved one, you need to be flexible and non-attached to whether or not they will like, dislike, accept, or reject what you offer. With the dissolution or breakdown of the Earth elements, there is no convention to stand on, save the convention of the value of pure service.

That said, there are a few things worth avoiding for their benefit. This I mention in the context of reducing pain and agitation.

In the discussion of hydration, I mentioned sugared drinks. These not only make us thirsty. The sugar will leach out nutrients and weaken us. It can even heighten pain. Thus, all things with refined flours and sugar are best kept to a minimum – if at all.

Eliminate nightshade plants such as potatoes, tomatoes, eggplant, and peppers. Because of their sodium-potassium ratios, they make a person's nervous system fire faster. As pain receptors are stimulated more frequently, people feel more pain, even if their condition is not getting worse. This phenomenon also holds true for eating bananas. Along with pain, they can even worsen agitation.

What to offer?

Of course, there is one contingent within the hospice community that would say that whatever the person wants, give them. Now is not the time to decide that grandma needs to become a vegetarian, etc... But, many of our food choices have contributed to our condition, our pain, and our agitation. And, even if you make a suggestion to change what foods are offered, they may adamantly want to stick with what is familiar, regardless of what it does. Be sensitive to maintain a balance in this.

In this light, here are some ideas of foods you may want to add or increase with respect to daily fare.

Try to think of light, nutritious, warming foods; soups, stews, cooked grains and vegetables, lighter types of meat if meat is what is asked for. If something cold or sweet is wanted, wee if things like apple sauce and fruit compotes are acceptable. And know that all of this will change – and change again.

And then one day, when they have not been eating very much at all, they make a request for a special meal, many of their old favorites and they eat on that day more than they have in weeks. And, you become convinced that they are "finally" on the mend. They are recovering.

In truth, more often than not, for them, this is their last supper. It serves many purposes. It brings people together. It lightens the mood. And it provides the calories and strength that is needed in their dying process.

Of course, we can always hope that this meal signifies remission or recovery. But I have seen too many people have their optimism shattered in the rapid decline after such a meal. Somewhere between optimism and dread there is the mind that lovingly stands witness and celebrates the moment as it is. Start there. Then support whatever comes next.

Beyond nutrition and hydration, attending to the physicality of the dying person's body becomes more and more of an issue as they become less mobile, stay in sitting, then finally lying positions for prolonged periods of time.

Throughout these external bodily changes, bathing goes from being in a tub, to being sponged down. Going beyond bathing to provide good hygiene and comfort, there is also massage.

MASSAGE

Many hospices have nurses or volunteers who offer one form of massage or another to clients. Some forms offered are more physical (like Swedish styles), others energetic (such as shiatsu and Reiki). As one approaches immanency, the dying person, who may have accepted and enjoyed a more physical massage in the early stages of decline may find this form of massage irritating and may even increase levels of pain or agitation. Massage, especially on the feet, elicit more agitation as the elements of the body dissolve into each other. When I mentioned lubrication earlier, I mentioned that massage with oils was also very helpful. It feeds the skin, keeps it moist and supple, thus there is less breakdown of the skin as a result. But, as the person becomes more bedbound, this may become impractical on all sorts of level. However, the one area that I would recommend to keep oiling with a quality vegetable oil (sesame, sunflower, safflower, olive) is the abdomen. This does not have to be done vigorous. But, just rubbing oil on to this area will help with bowel function, hence the bloating, gas, and constipation that is exacerbated by so many medications. Beyond oil to this region, the forms of massage best received in the latter stages of dying are the energetic ones, such as Reiki, meridian stroking, and so on. These types of massage require the lightest of touch and help to smooth out the subtle energy channels of the acupuncture meridian system and the chakra network. And, in the final days, massage of the scalp is especially useful. This can be done, even by just brushing the hair. Besides the comfort that this provides, it brings the dying person's attention to the crown of their head which, when dying actually occurs, helps them to be more conscious and possibly exit from the crown chakra. In Tibetan tradition, they actually prepare a salve of cowry shell and honey that they put on the crown of the head to draw the consciousness upwards towards the crown. Short of doing this, brushing or gentle strokes to the very top of the head will greatly assist the dying one.

MEDICATION

When speaking earlier about medications and some of their unwelcome side-effects, I am not saying that all medications should be eliminated. There are life situations and conditions that plainly will cause much suffering if medication is suspended or some kind of palliative medicine, whether it be an herb or drug is not offered.

With respect to common medically prescribed or recommended pain medications, these are generally masterfully tended to by hospice nurses. They probably know more about titrating medications better than any other health care provider. They truly are angels of mercy. That is why it is such a shame when families and their attending physicians hold out to the very end before calling hospice in. Not knowing and not accepting the dying process as a natural part of life, I have counseled many who think that by accepting death or talking about or preparing for the death of their loved one that they are giving up on them or somehow willing it to happen. This simply is not true and cannot happen. What is true, though, is that if we fail to learn how death comes and what it will look like, many opportunities to offer a more compassionate care to our loved ones will pass by and we shall be scrambling with more fear and anxiety than is really necessary in this time. All that said, please remember that you can always call hospice in and if they think you or your loved one are inappropriate for hospice care and can still pursue more curative means, they will tell you. You can always go off hospice then come back on when the time is more appropriate.

When I mention properly titrating medications, I mean to say that when a nurse knows how to administer pain medications properly, the dose hits the pain receptors, but does not flood the system. Thus a person can be lucid or at least clear and relaxed on morphine, etc.. One does not have to be in oblivion or almost comatose although when pain is so extreme, that reaction to pain meds is hard to avoid.

So, with a better diet and hydration, an occasional appropriate massage, and proper levels of medication, pain and agitation can be kept to a minimum through the dying process. And at the same time, one has to know that what this looks like from day to day will change as one approaches their final moments.

TRANSCENDING AND TRANSFORMING PAIN

As pain is subjective, one cannot wholly use physical markers as to what pain person is experiencing. So much of this comes down to their emotional state and spiritual preparedness. And there are times when no matter how hard care givers try to create the optimal (yet ever changing) conditions to ease the pain, suffering goes on. This is because of the fact that as we still thinking of ourselves as our body rather than – as I explained earlier – having our body - we remain identified with our pain. It insults our personhood – and we resist.

So, how can we assist someone to overcome this common, illusory identification? The answer lies in giving pain a transcendent meaning and goal.

In clients I have seen this done through various forms of prayer. Every tradition has powerful and inspiring words or verbal formulas; incantations that can be used to inspire courage and overcome adversity. In *Perfect Endings*, I tell of a women who used the Lord's Prayer as a mantra. She repeated it over and over again as a way of rising above her pain, keeping her mind focused on inspiring words. She preferred this over medication. It kept her mind focused, but content. Even to towards the end, she was thus able to be more present with her family. In many respects, it was her salvation and final teaching to all of her children of the power of prayer.

In another case, I instructed a client in the Taking and Sending meditation in Buddhism, known as *tong len*. Taking and sending means to take on the suffering of others and giving them your joy and happiness. This counter-intuitive meditation is a powerful antidote to excessive self preoccupation and builds a tremendous reservoir of compassion for others. I have taught this meditation to many people with chronic pain and degenerative diseases such as cancer. The premise is built on the notion that is te heart of Buddhist philosophy; that we are all basically good and the greatest pleasure we get in life is seeing and/or offering whatever we can to make others in our life happy. In essence, as spiritual beings having a human experience, we are altruistic at our core. Thus, when we are in extreme pain or pain that no medication seems to do enough to abate, think of others.

Imagine that there are those around you who have a similar illness or level of pain that they are experiencing. Knowing the misery that you have, it is not hard to have strong empathy for others suffering the same. As much as you no longer want to suffer, you know that they, too, no longer want to suffer. Focusing on them, as you breathe in, imagine that you are breathing in all of their pain and suffering. The buck stops here. The buck stops with you. You want your pain to be the sum total of all of their pain. You want your pain to be the end of pain for yourself, but especially for others. As you breathe in let their pain blend in with your pain. See it dissolving into your pain. And, as you breathe out, imagine that any relief you can conjure in your mind, you send out to them. See white or deep blue light pouring out of every pore of your body in every direction, going into each and every being who is suffering just like you. Imagine that they are receiving medications, a doctor's visit, the loving hands of another taking away their pain. Breathe in the pain, breathe out the relief. Do this again and again with the thought or wish, "May my pain be the end of this kind of pain in all places and times for each and every being. Let it stop here and now."

In doing such a meditation, I have seen amazing transformations. It has eased pain and brought its practitioner into a greater state of peace and grace.

HOLDING ON and LETTING GO

As mentioned earlier in the medical and philosophical discussion of the dying process as understood in the east, at the moment of our birth, a wise doctor can take the pulses of a baby and know exactly when it is that they will die. This may be hard for us to accept. But based on the intelligent design of divine force coupled with the aggregate of what we have and have not learned from previous existences, we come into this life, not as a tabula rasa, a blank slate, but a slate whose design demands of us to learn what we can to bring forth within ourselves the light, the awakened state, that is a testimony to our spiritual beingness.

This does not happen in a vacuum. It happens within the context of the world into which we find ourselves born. It is our field of play and everyone and everything around us is a participant. What that means is that we, too, are participants in the lives of others. We are part of the field in which they will play, will learn, will transform themselves over the course of their lives. We are in this together. We may feel lonely, but in truth, we never are, never were, and never will be alone.

Thus it is that when we die, we do die in accordance with how we have lived. It is our own amazing journey. But, that journey that we take plays a role in the lives of those who we have touched in any number of ways over the course of our lives. And it is hard to determine who will feel the impact of your dying the most; those who are closest to you, close to the center of the mandala of which you are the epicenter, or someone who you made an impression upon in years past.

Thus, depending on where they are, who they are, and what they have to learn at the time, your dying will play a role in their transformation. For your spouse, it may be the lesson of realizing how much you meant to them or a call to become more independent. To a friend, it may be a wake-up call to not be so materialistic. To a son or daughter, it may teach them of the fragileness of life and the value of getting on and doing what life is calling them to do. The point here is that unless we willfully take our own lives, we shall die when we are suppose to die and part and parcel of our dying will be contained the many lessons that others need to glean from our dying. As beings who are part of this universe, how could it be any other way?

A fellow hospice social worker once told me of a gentleman who had been languishing for months in the latter stages of his disease. He commented to her that he did not know why God would not let him just die. What was the point in all this suffering, this lingering at the edge. After all, he had tried to do all he could to please God. He recited to her a verse that he repeated to remind himself to do so.

Knowing the verse well, she told him that he had forgotten then end of the verse, which end in "and accept my will." After doing all he could, he need to accept the will of his God. That was the final instruction.

Having an epiphany of this as the missing key, he relaxed. And by the next day, he was gone.

From a Buddhist point of view, I would look at this incident as an example of right timing. His lingering had a purpose. He was not finished with whatever the lesson was that he needed to get before he passed. And, once received, his seemingly stalled journey proceeded.

Thus I take issue with the premise that asserts the possibility of a person prolonging their life because they are "holding on," or not "letting go." Rather, I would contend that there are final lessons being learned that may be happening in a person's dreams, while in a coma, a seeming state of dementia, or just lying motionless but alert in bed month after month; lessons that we may never be privy to, but are, nonetheless, bringing resolution and completion to lighten their load for what comes next.

Bearing this in mind, in the process of going into rapid decline and the immanency of death itself, there can be an attachment to one's life force that creates psychic discomfort. From the outside, this appears as agitation. And, as agitation has probably been met with some medication up to this point, it stands to reason in the stress of witnessing such so close to the gates of death, that a final push of morphine or whatever would seem warranted, perhaps even humane. But, to assist the person to overcome attachment that may be the cause of such agitation, there are still some things that can be done before adding more medication at a time when clarity would be preferred.

Hospice nurses and others in attendance of the dying have noted that if you role a person on to their right side, they seem to calm down. It stops the agitation and they are able to pass more peacefully. While the reason for this is unknown in western medical terms, it is explainable in Ayurvedic terms and from the tradition of yoga.

As mentioned earlier, we have subtle channels in our bodies that are associated with the acupuncture meridian system and the chakra vortex and its associated grid. The chakra grid has channels that have associated with them our various emotions. Primarily, there are three major channels. In the center, running anterior to our spine there is a channel associated with confusion. On the left side there is a channel associated with anger and irritability. On the right side, there is a channel associated with attachment. Thus, when lying the person on their right side, you are blocking or inhibiting the flow in the channels associated with attachment. Thus, they are able to let go more easily.

That said, moving a person in their time of immanence can be quite traumatic for them. Tibetan teachers say that moving a person at that time can feel like an earthquake is happening within them. In such a fragile state with so many energetic systems struggling be in their state of letting go into death, it may be best just to leave the person as they are.

However, **this blocking of the right channels can also be accomplished by packing the person's right nostril and right ear with cotton.**

What you will notice when you do this is that their agitation, displayed by their labored breathing, begins to adjust. It changes and slows down. What will also help from that point on is to approach the person from their left side and give them any direction, word of love, or encouragement into their left ear.

To be willing to do this as a final act of compassion as a caregiver takes great strength. This may be something which you cannot bring yourself to do. But, please understand that in doing so, you will not be shortening your beloved dying friend's life. This is not an act of euthanasia. It is a simple act of assisting in the lightening of the subtle psychic force of attachment. With less discomfort from the agitation created by such, you will be assisting them to set off from this life with more grace.

Such attachment-type agitation does not happen for everyone. You or the one who you stand witness for may not go through this experience. Regardless of how the dying person's final breath comes as they slip into the concentrated state after physical death, if you have been able to apply what you have learned here in as many ways as are useful and possible, you will have been able to be in the presence of death and offer the person who lies still before you acts of compassion that are beneficial for them, and you.

This will bind the two of you in a legacy that you will carry and pass on through the course of your own life. It will be a legacy of an amazing journey shared.

THE GIFT OF SHAMARA

In many of the classes I teach on healing, a point that I often come back to is that no matter how many beautiful books and inspired teachers there are whose purpose for being is to impart the wisdom we need to lead healthy, happy, and inspired lives, most of us learn from disaster.

There is probably no more excruciating a moment for a parent than to hold the lifeless body of their own child. I would not wish this on anyone. Yet, this is how it was for me. And, it changed everything. Looking upon and holding the truth of impermanence in my own hands, a smugness of my privileged upbringing dropped away. The zealot way in which I held to truths about life, health, spirituality was replaced with awe and humility in the face of watching the world around me become resplendent with miracles and the deep loving care of teachers, friends, even strangers.

Although I document a number of incidences where I could feel a guiding or protecting presence, I am not so bold as to say this was or is in these times, Shamara. What Lama Ole and other have told me of Dewachen is that as beings there become enlightened they do what more enlightened and fully enlightened beings do; they help the rest of us. That being the case, I know that Shamara has been helping me, been a guiding light in my life.

Everything that I share here, the story, the theoretical presentation, the exercise, the practical suggestions to prepare oneself and another in the decline and immanency of dying, along with my reflections come as a result of Shamara being born, living her short life, and passing away. To think of a child that was born to the sound of prayers, the fact that it was when hearing prayers that she looked and seemed most peaceful, that she died after being in the presence of a spiritual teaching, and that her death was attended to in the most auspicious way possible, and - most importantly - the fact that the telling of her story either in conversation or through print has always transformed the listener for the better, makes me feel that Shamara never was an ordinary child. She was and remains a teacher to us all. She reminds us of the fragile and precious nature of our lives And her death and transformation from the yoga of phowa teaches us that there is not one moment in our lives that is ever wasted.

Looking at my life to date, I would say that it has been amazing. I have the habit of liking to break words down in different ways. If I break the word "amazing" down, the prefix "a" in Latin means "from." Then there is the word "maze." We often feel and most certainly become trapped in the maze of our own design. Shamara helped to pull me away from the phantasm, the maze that I thought was life into a vaster, richer, more loving world. She amazed and amazes me.

My hope is that Shamara's life, legacy, and lessons will bring amazement into your life.

Have an amazing journey. May you, too, be reborn into a Pure Land.

GLOSSARY

Avalokitesvara (ah-vah-lo-kee-tesh-vah-ra) - Sanskrit name for the Bodhisattva of Compassion who was originally one of the main disciples of the Buddha. In Tibetan he is called Chenrezig.

Bodhisattva (bo-dhee-saht-vah) - an adept of the Mahayana path who can no longer fall into the confusion of mundane reality (samsara) and is committed to the liberation of all beings caught in such.

Chenrezig (chehn-ray-zig) - the Tibetan name for the Bodhisattva of Compassion. His mantra is OM MANI PEME HUNG (Ohm-mah-nee-peh-meh-hoong) [Tibetan].

Damaru (dah-mah-ru) a hand-held, double-sided drum used in certain Buddhist practices.

Dewachen (deh-wah-chen) - the "pure land" of the Amitahba Buddha, the Buddha of Discriminating Aware-ness. It is also called the Western Pure Land and is the easiest of the pure lands to be reborn into from our plane of existence.

Dharma (dahr-mah) - the truth or "way things are" as taught by the Buddha. There are worldly dharmas or relative truths and ultimate dharma, which is what the Buddha taught about the nature of reality.

Dharmadhatu (dahr-mah-dah-too) - in this context, one of the local centers under the umbrella of Vajradhatu, the organization set up under the guidance of the Vajracarya Chogyam Trungpa Rinpoche.

Four Noble Truths - the first teaching of the Buddha after His enlightenment. Essentially, these four truths are that regardless of whether or not we see it clearly, life based on anything but the truth of how reality actually is, is suffering; that the cause of this suffering is our ego clinging to our misperceptions of reality; that there is a way out of this suffering; and that way is the Middle Way, or learning how to see things as they truly are and to act and live in accordance with that truth.

Kagyu (kah-gyoo) - one of the four main lineages of Tibetan Buddhism. It is also called the Practice Lineage or Mishap Lineage. Its main teacher is His Holiness the Gyalwa Karmapa.

Kagyu Samye (sam-yeh) Ling - one of the first and foremost meditation centers in the West, located in Eskdalemuir, Scotland. Originally started by Ven. Chogyam Trungpa Rinpoche and Akong Rinpoche.

Kalu (kah-loo) Rinpoche - one of the great yogis of the Kagyu Lineage. It is currently a young boy training at his own monastery in Sonada, India.

Karma (kahr-mah) - the law of cause and effect. It is what we experience from our actions. However, it does not imply that everything is predestined. We affect our future karma by how we respond to the circumstances and situations we find ourselves in as a result of our previous actions. Thus, although we cannot change the past, how we deal with the present will have a direct effect on what we will experience in the future.

Karmapa (kahr-mah-pah) - also called Gyalwa Karmapa. Karmapa means "he who performs the activity of a Buddha" or, briefly, Man of Action. He is the main teacher and center of the Kagyu Lineage, the first of the reincarnates of Tibet to return as the same being lifetime after lifetime. He is called the Knower of the Three Times, because his energy, power and awareness make him beyond time and capable of seeing into and acting on behalf of sentient beings in all places and times. He is currently in his 17th incarnation. His sacred mantra or chant is KARMAPA CHENO (Kahr-mah-pah Chay-noh).

Karma Triyana Dharmachakra - The main U.S. seat of His Holiness the Gyalwa Karmapa, located in Woodstock, New York.

Khenpo Karthar Rinpoche (ken-poh kahr-tahr) - abbot of Karma Triyana Dharmachakra, the seat of His Holiness the Gyalwa Karmapa in America. Khenpo means abbot and Karthar is an abbreviation of his full name, Karma Tharchen. He is regarded as one of the finest Dharma masters in the West and is respected by all lineages for his vast knowledge of the vehicles and commentaries of Buddhism.

Lama (lah-ma)- a person who is recognized for his/her meditative accomplishment and is bestowed with this title as a distinction and also as an acknowledgement of the ability to teach others.

Lama Ole Nydahl - One of the first western students, along with his wife, Hannah, of His Holiness the 16th Gyalwa Karmapa. His Holiness directed Ole and Hannah to many teachers in Asia and then entrusted Ole to teach throughout Europe and begin the process of opening up centers in America and around the world. His teacher is Tenga Rinpoche who has directed Ole to teach Phowa or the conscious dying practice of Tibetan Buddhism to as many students as possible. He now acts under the direction of the Ven. Shamar Rinpoche.

Mikyo Dorje (mih-kyoh dohr-jay) - the 8th historical Gyalwa Karmapa.

Ngodrup Burkhar (noo-droop boor-kar) - one of the foremost translators for Kagyu teachers in America and Asia.

Phowa (poh-wah) - the special meditative practice that is for the transference of consciousness at the time of dying. The transference that is focused on is where the being's consciousness leaves the body from the crown of the head and enters into Dewachen, the Pure Land of the Amitabha Buddha.

Pure Land - a celestial realm which is a manifestation of and presided over by an enlightened being. Beings reborn into a pure land are given the opportunity to do spiritual practice without distraction and with the blessing of whichever enlightened being's pure land it is.

Refuge - a formal ceremony one undergoes to be considered an official member of the Buddhist community. One is taking "refuge" in beings who exemplify our enlightened potential, their teachings (Dharma) and the community which practices in accordance with these teachings.

Rinpoche (rihn-poh-shay) - means Precious One, usually an incarnate or "tulku" who has consciously returned to a realm of relative beings to teach the Dharma and help them to reach enlightenment.

Samaya (sah-mai-yah) - a sacred bond of commitment to a teacher and the teachings he or she gives.

Sangha (sahn-gah) - the community of those who practice and study the teachings of the Buddha.

Sharmapa (shahr-mah-pah) - also called His Eminence Shamar Rinpoche. Shamar Rinpoche is one of the Four Regents of the Kagyu Lineage. He is an emanation of the Amitabha Buddha and has reincarnated throughout time along with His Holiness the Gyalwa Karmapa. He is currently in his 13th incarnation.

Stupa - a three dimensional symbolic representation of the path to enlightenment and enlightenment itself. The historical Buddha was supposedly to have seen this form in space.

USEFUL ADDRESSES

To learn more about the teachings of Kunzig Shamar Rinpoche, contact:

BodhiPath – Main American Center
449 Galloping Path
Natural Bridge, VA 24578
www.bodhipath.org
Phone: 540-463-5117

To learn more about the teachings and schedule of Ven. Khenpo Karthar Rinpoche, contact:

Karma Triyana Dharmachakra
352 Meads Mountain Road
Woodstock, NY 12498
Phone: 914-679-5906

To learn more about the teachings of Ole Nydahl and his courses on Phowa, contact:

Diamond Way Buddhist Center
110 Merced Ave.
San Francisco, CA 94127
Email:
SanFrancisco@diamondway-center.org
Phone: 415-661-6030
        or

Diamond Way Europe Center
Gut Hochreute
D-87509 Immenstadt
GERMANY
www.europe-center.org
europecenter@diamondway-center.org
Phone: 49-(8323)96830

ALSO: To have loved ones put on a list for phowa to be done for them, go to:
http://phowa.diamondway-buddhism.org/web/

For information about SIDS (Sudden Infant Death Syndrome), contact:
American SIDS Institute
528 Raven Way
Naples, FL 34110
www.sids.org
Phone: 239-431-5425

For information about local hospice services, contact:
National Hospice &
Palliative Care Organization (NHPCO)
1731 King Street Suite 100
Alexandria, VA 22314
www.nhpco.org
Phone: 703-837-1500

To contact the author and his family, write to:
Robert and Melanie Sachs
P.O. Box 13753
San Luis Obispo, CA 93406
Email: mandrsachs@earthlink.net
Telephone: 866-303-3321 or 805-543-9291

(To order a signed, first edition copy of
Rebirth Into Pure Land, contact Robert
at passion8@earthlink.net, call 805-543-9291 or write
him at P.O Box 13753,
San Luis Obispo, CA 93406)

Made in the USA
Charleston, SC
09 March 2016